The
Wellman
Stories

Passions, Professions and Politics in Iowa

Margaret J. Hansen

The Wellman Stories

Published by Nighthawk Press
Taos, New Mexico

ISBN: 978-1-7334483-0-7

Cover photo taken near
Alburnett, Iowa, by David Chase

Author photo by Kathleen Brennan

NIGHTHAWK PRESS
TAOS, NEW MEXICO

The
Wellman
Stories

The Wellman Stories

For Karen.

*For our friends, patients, dear ones
and Iowa*

What's This About Wellman?

KAREN: *You are really going to write our Wellman stories?*

MARGARET: *I am. Well, best I can anyway.*

KAREN: *I hope you will tell the whole story without shilly-shallying around like you often do. You've got to tell it all.*

MARGARET: *I will. Remember, there's a lot to these stories...about who we met, why we stayed, all that we learned...before the changes came.*

KAREN: *OK. But you must.*

Wellman. Such a prosperous and propitious name. Don't you think? With sincerity and integrity? Certainly a healer's delight.

That name is partly what drew the two of us to the small town of Wellman, Iowa, in the late 1980s. It's decades later now and I have a few stories for you...scenes from what, at a glance, is either a bucolic, quiet, peaceful place or a backward, prejudiced place of no opportunity — except from the seat of a giant air-conditioned, CD-playing, GPS-driven tractor.

We begin as newly minted chiropractors in our middle age in a newly minted relationship, one of us from city/university life, the other from the dull edge of suburbia. We have absent families and financial coffers that have been licked dry. So we decide to take advantage of an inexpensive beginning. We hone our professional skills on a surprisingly diverse, albeit nearly colorless, patient base. And before we know it we are serving this country community that historically goes first to the chiropractor, before the medical doctor. We have become theirs. Their outsiders: *those girls, those ladies, those doctors.* Our advantage is being able to hear each person's story afresh, without the close-quartered familiarity and preconceptions of the community.

In return, we have the time and creative necessity to develop skills that might never have manifested in a time- and insurance-driven city practice. We have a place to become well women ourselves.

As you cogitate on how two professional women might end up in such an unlikely place, reflect on one of our early clues. A photo from the 1930s or forties hangs in the University of Iowa's Hospital Museum. It is a grainy black-and-white portrait of Beth L. Wellman, PhD, daughter of the original Wellman family. She is a bespectacled, intelligent-eyed behavioral psychologist, known for studying and writing about the significance of environment on the intelligence of children.

Here is an educated woman whose name and background connect her to this town — back when freight trains rumbled through the surrounding bounty of farmland. It was a thriving home to a turkey factory, two lumberyards, two or three hardware stores, five or six churches, at least a couple of bars, several cafés and to the woman who proclaimed she'd made and sold enough apple, rhubarb, raspberry, pecan and lemon-merengue pies to lay crust-to-crust down the highway and back to the next town six miles away. We think maybe a scholarly woman named Wellman portends something good for us here.

There is no chance they ever refer to us as genuine Wellmanites. Yet, we cultivate an accomplished, yet fragile, symbiotic coexistence. Then, unbecoming, corrupting, disparaging forces insinuate themselves, one-by-one, plucking the threads of our connection and we have to leave.

Come with me on a little journey. First I have to introduce you to our origins at Palmer College. Then I promise to take you with us into the countryside to see for yourselves. I'll skimp on journalistic research and avoid the deadly prose and sharp-angled graphs of a time-consuming sociological study and just share stories. Stories about people we met, about what we learned, about our experience in alternative healthcare in the late twentieth century in a small American Midwestern town at the time of its fading influence, during the heyday of warp-speed corporate agriculture and a rising wave of new influences. You'll see.

Will this Kinesiology skill really be able to unlock and reveal subconscious truth?

The Beginning

Out in front of a two-story red brick apartment house in Davenport, Iowa, near the Palmer College of Chiropractic campus. Moving boxes scrawled with magic marker destinations sit on the grass. Guys haul furniture and women direct the flow. Two of us, in sweatshirts and work gloves, have a brief opening conversation.

MARGARET: *It's good to finally meet you. I've seen you around campus and in the clinic. Do you suppose our hosts thought it was finally OK to invite us to the same gathering?*

KAREN: *Probably since they're leaving town and want all hands on deck. I've seen you playing softball.*

MARGARET: *Want a ride to the taco place later?*

1984 is the year of our movie-actor president Ronald Reagan's reelection. He's big on freedom fighters and deregulation. Tina Turner sings *What's Love Got to Do With It?* American scientists disagree with French scientists about who discovered the AIDS virus.

I quietly finish my educational to-do list while the outer world boils over with trendy big hair and shoulder pads, break dancing and hip-hop, the politically ignored AIDS epidemic and soaring interest rates. First is my undergraduate biology degree in 1983. It had an unguided beginning twenty years earlier with my plan to take a class from every building at the University of Iowa, sixty miles west of here in the Iowa heartland.

Now I'm on my final endurance run for a chiropractic diploma — the postgraduate degree that my dad offered to pay for, except when I chose this one. It's taken thirteen years from beginning to now. Travels and jobs intervened. These are merry euphemisms for romantic, idealistic or naïve ventures. I'm back in Davenport — the manufacturing river town where I grew up, where the Mississippi River flows west, home to two redeeming features besides Mark Twain's river stories — the Quad City Symphony and Palmer College, the "Fountainhead of Chiropractic."

Karen Zakar (rhymes with Baker) and I are introduced that spring by our Palmer friends, the newly graduated Dr. Denise and her husband Mark, who are indulging in a common Iowa social practice. What happens is the couple is leaving town and they throw a party. Suddenly they invite all their friends together for the first time. "Hey, here you all are now, but we've got to go." In this case the party is to help them load their moving truck and then celebrate over gluey tacos at a fairly wretched Mexican restaurant across the river in Moline. Karen and I sit across from each other in a grimy booth, still in our moving clothes.

She is finishing her fourth-year classes and senior clinic. But, much to the surprise of our now distant friends, we get along. We spend the humid, green summer canoeing tiny landlocked Lake George, which has no whitewater unless the wind is blowing at thirty miles per hour. We loll about the lake in two-piece bathing suits, paddling the edges, the middles and the edges again, admiring our newly acquainted bodies in a rented aluminum canoe. She, a former oceanographer, tells me about that tiny, soft, bright-green, disc-shaped water plant called duckweed that grows in still water.

Her short blonde hair curls above shining eyes, more turquoise than duckweed-colored. Her bird arms and glam legs soak up the available photons in the thick torpid air. I have straight poky brown hair and some sort of skimpy suit — easy to slip off for a little skinny-dipping around the corner, under the overhanging trees.

We fall in love that carefree summer. She is in her early forties and I'm in my late thirties. Her military family abjures any warmth or connection; my family is fractured by alcohol, religion and suicide. We reveal fragments of these stories before skimming through successes, betrayals and embarrassments of our personal and academic pasts so we can get to our ever-dawning theories and insights.

Life is quieter than the previous decades. Disco, psychedelics, weird drinking and the Harvey Milk era are passed. She takes Reiki class and has an intense meeting with the higher realms of Love. Lying on the grass at Scott County Park, I receive my first treatment as she lifts my spirit on a flamboyant trip of exhilaration and allows the anxiety and desperation of past emotions to ooze as energetic gray gunk from my knees and ankles.

"You know this is all new for me," she says. "The scientist part has to observe in a new way, since wellness is not a double blind experiment or linear data collection over time."

"Right," I say, "It's often a matter of 'Does that feel better or not?' To which, my answer at this moment is *I feel great!* Even considering that I'm just an individual case study, with multiple unrepeatable variables. Here, does this help your transition?" I kiss her lips, cheek and earlobe as we draw close.

She smiles. "I believe it does."

Returning to our professional realities and aspirations, I see that Karen's student clinic practice is thriving with middle-aged to elderly men and young people from the gay community. Even as our intimacy grows easy and comfortable, we readily assume the cloak of professional demeanor as we put on our white clinic jackets. We navigate personal, public and professional borders seamlessly, as will be the necessary custom throughout our professional lives.

We administer professional care to our patients and to each other as student doctors. Our goal is to support the structural integrity of the body so we don't have to rely on pills to mask symptoms. These are our first baby steps merging the assessment of a patient's presenting history and physical symptoms with intuition and art.

I treat her inflamed sciatic nerve, acquired from sitting in the terrible plastic chairs in the new classrooms. (How can this be in Chiro school?) As the doctor, I provide what is called a Basic adjustment, a gentle lift of her right ischium / sit bone as she lies prone on the table with bolsters under her hips and lower legs. I massage each vertebral level and she breathes her spine into relaxation. This technique comes from the Logan school of treating the spine upward from the sacral base.

She treats my neck strain with an atlas toggle, realigning that topmost bone in my spine. She, as the doctor, superimposes her wrists over my neck at the base of my skull as I lie on my side, then quickly snaps together and releases her elbows directing a quick force to drop my head and the headpiece of the table and oscillate my atlas into alignment. This method comes from the Palmer school of treating the spine from the top down.

It's a summer of expansion, insight and romantic adventure — even in the movies like *Ghostbusters*, *Back to the Future* and *Romancing the Stone*.

The Body stores a lifetime of emotional memory.

Our Origins

An evening at Margaret's studio apartment a block from Palmer. She serves student organic fare: black beans, rice, wilted greens and onions, chunks of goat cheddar.

MARGARET: *You know, over the years I have matriculated here, I've learned some secrets about this place.*

KAREN: *OK, tell me one.*

MARGARET: *Well, for example, you know the top vertebra of the spine is the atlas — named after the Greek god Atlas who, with arms extended, holds the earth in the heavens. And you know it supports the skull and encircles the spinal cord with bony protection as it leaves the brain to innervate the body.*

KAREN: *I believe I know this well ... but that's a good description and the basis for why we pay such close attention to its positioning.*

MARGARET: *Exactly. And yet I heard there were early experiments done on volunteer patients who had their atlases repeatedly adjusted from the wrong side. And these people had all kinds of pains, with postural and gait anomalies, headaches and digestive problems. It's just a mirage in my memory now, remembering papers being cleared out of closets when the new library was built. I don't even know if they got preserved. ... You want anymore of this?*

KAREN: *Hmm, interesting. People must have been dedicated to volunteer for that. ... I think your vegetarian diet is making me fat.*

In Chiropractic Theory class we learn to prize the idea that healthy nerves actuate cells and tissues. We learn that a misaligned vertebra causes pain or malfunction or, as the overly simplistic metaphor goes, "steps on the garden hose," diminishing the nerve impulse. I sing her the goofy song that my now-graduated friend Elmer and I used to sing with gusto:

> Pressure on the Brain,
> It is such a pain,
> Oh how we hate it,
> Presshhure o-on the Brrrainnn.

And choruses like, "We can relieve it," "You can believe it!"

Karen has come to this school because it's the "fountainhead" of chiropractic; I'm here because it's my hometown — even if I said I'd never return.

The "father" of chiropractic was Daniel David Palmer, right here in downtown Davenport. He restored the hearing for one of his first patients by walloping a neck bone into place. His son Bartlett Joshua, BJ, advanced the philosophy, perfected adjusting methods and was one of the first to use X-rays and a heat-sensing device to study the alignment of spinal bones. He donated much of his vast Asian artifacts collection to Davenport's Putnam Museum. That's where, in my senior year in high school, as volunteer docent, I found a book with a fabulous red, black and gold coiled dragon to use as the model for the thirty-foot monster we painted to surround and protect the queen's throne at a senior high dance. BJ also ran a local media empire —

WOC radio/TV station here in Davenport, which supposedly stands for World of Chiropractic, and WHO, the Midwest powerhouse 50,000-watt clear channel radio in Des Moines, which stands for With Hands Only.

The Palmer mansion and college, at the top of the Brady Street hill, loom above the tallest trees over the expanse of the Mississippi valley. On the clinic's walls, along the tiled hallways, are many of BJ's maxims. They are easy to see in their bold, polished, triangular letters as you ascend the time-smoothed granite steps with their wooden handrails:

THE POWER THAT MADE THE BODY HEALS THE BODY.

CHIROPRACTIC IS NOT DESIGNED TO MAKE YOU INSTANTLY FEEL BETTER; IT'S DESIGNED TO MAKE YOU INSTANTLY HEAL BETTER.

WE MAKE A LIVING BY WHAT WE GET, BUT A LIFE BY WHAT WE GIVE.

BJ has been gone since the early sixties. The school has some old-timers who knew him well and are infused with his guiding philosophical energy. They are simultaneously stuck in that time warp and cannot provide new leadership in the art of chiropractic. A few of them are misogynist pricks. To learn the most innovative techniques being developed we pay extra and go to weekend seminars, which is where we each discover Applied Kinesiology — its brilliant muscle, organ, topography relationships and the ease of communicating with a body through muscle testing.

Summer quarter and lolling about the lake have come to an end by mid-August. Karen and I have a last-of-the-summer kiss in the clinic room furthest from the front desk as a flurry of activity takes place in the hallway during the annual homecoming preparations. Goodbye Section Five, where no one can hear when she muscle tests and adjusts her patient with the Activator® — a little percussive instrument that sends a directed force along a desired path. These are not techniques in the curriculum.

Then, come September, I happily endure Karen's graduation with her. In the purple-and-gold-decorated auditorium with a Z last name she sits in the last seat of her class, all by herself on the aisle in a row of empty folding chairs. I sit directly across the aisle to keep her company and wink when she returns flushed and resplendent with her diploma.

Her immediate plans are to return to Washington State and work as the intake doc for the state's largest chiropractic practice. This means X-raying, then doing physical exams on six to eight new patients daily. "Goodbye, honey. We'll see each other soon."

My senior clinic begins. I have enough patients, inherited and new, between the Davenport clinic and the Rock Island clinic across the river, that I'll be able to fulfill my requirements. Right off the bat Karen's network brings me one of my first patients, a twenty-two-year-old woman who works in a factory in Moline. "I've just spent three days in the hospital," she says through her crooked mouth because the left side of her face is swollen. "No one has been able to determine what's wrong."

OK, ominous beginning, which we will discover is not an uncommon theme. I adjust her all-important atlas and show her how to stimulate lymphatic flow along her upper ribs. "Let's see you again this time next week," I say with affected confidence.

In a week she walks in and smiles. "Look at this!" And there it is, her cheerful nonasymmetric smile. Well, well, even though I was nervous all week, part of me knew it would be, could be, successful. Patient and doctor are proud.

Soon, it's my turn to graduate. Karen returns after eight months as part of that big-city chiropractic money machine. I pick her up at O'Hare in Chicago. "Hi, babe, welcome back. You look good — a little thin. Learn a lot?"

"Hi Honey. Well, I'm glad I did it, but glad it's done. I missed you."

It's now 1985 and thirteen years since my first matriculation, back in 1972. A lot happened between then and now. There was a beach romance with gardenia fragrances and diving pelicans in Sarasota before the bulldozers took over; New York chic, including chance visits with esteemed artists and a scotch-fueled night of Sapphic memoir, before the city was ravished by AIDS; trysts in London and Lisbon. There was moving back and forth between Iowa and New Mexico, several times; many jobs; two failed businesses — a restaurant and a movie production; two careers — one managing a natural foods grocery store, the other editing at the New Mexico Legislature and Sunstone Press; several relationships; plus completing that biology degree. Still, I tell Karen it took me so long because I was waiting for her to get here.

Today, I don the regal purple robe with golden hood over my silk shirt, antelope-colored gabardine pants and soft brown cowboy boots. On stage there is a swirl of royal regalia, majestic organ processional and much purple pontificating. Then, just like in Karen's ceremony last year, we are metaphorically patted on our mortarboard heads, told we will make great entrepreneurs and thrown to the winds.

As they read "Margaret Joan Hansen," I step onto the stage, exultant. My heart feels open wide, then my ears are flooded with a wild cheer from the balcony up to my right. Two of my school friends and Karen have made a giant sign with my extremely old matriculation number (#28809) and draped it over three balcony seats! The emperor delivers the leather-bound parchment with my name embossed in gold.

In that moment I accept it all — my imperfect and itinerant past, the inglorious yet noble aspects of our alma mater and, simultaneously, the considered meaning of my diploma and the accompanying Hippocratic oath.

The to-do lists are complete. Where shall we go from here?

In a Balance session we explore subconscious beliefs to re-place acquired negative irrational beliefs with affirming, Self-actualizing ones.

Into the Corn!

The "Hilton," our $195-a-month tiny trailer with real insulation, sits on a green hillside out past the Iowa City airport. Last fall, after graduation, I planted a pin oak tree lifted over the fence from the nursery where it sat haggard and desolate at the end of the season. Early this spring I cleared a rectangle in front of the wrought iron steps for Karen to plant a thirty-cent packet of wildflower mix. The flowers are coming up but someone from the trailer across the way has already backed over the shiny green pin oak.

It's a late afternoon in May, 1986. We sit at the gray-and-red boomerang-patterned Formica table between dainty windows and wood-paneled walls, bathed in home-made pizza aromas from the teensy stove.

KAREN: *Be good to get out of here, for sure. No more possum peering between my legs from the end of the bed while I'm immersed in my space alien mystery story. We can go pick up Paws and get moved in.*

MARGARET: *We can leave all these feral cats and game day flyovers. I hope Chester will not talk all day.*

KAREN: *We can get our state board exams passed and do the thing we've studied for. Have you signed up for that EK Class?*

MARGARET: *Starts in August. Educational Kinesiology. Hope it's more alive than its egghead name.*

We're bobbing along into the cornfields that surround Iowa City's particular reach and character. After graduation we've come to live in Iowa City because it's friendly and familiar. Assessing the realities of our hard-won independence and the fact that neither of us has a State of Iowa license to practice yet, we get university jobs to accommodate the rent and our student loans. Karen is testing water quality at the hygienic lab for the state's rivers, wells and streams. (It's not good.) She and the other techs watch this new show called *Oprah* during their breaks.

I am also in a white lab coat with a name tag at the University of Iowa Hospitals and Clinics in the Pathology Lab, because there is no call for a chiropractic viewpoint in any medical or research department. During my orientation, I am introduced to a giant administrative wall chart of hospital hierarchy. My position is in the bottom right hand corner of the chart, barely above the margin and below an ascending order of technicians, administrators, nurses, doctors, hierophants, a few priestesses and, at the top, the power-wielding emperors. The insurance companies are not designated, just the unmentioned milieu that surrounds us all.

This past winter, we've been getting to know each other in the close quarters of our thirty-foot Hilton trailer. Our multitude of books line the center room making it smaller, but much warmer, out here at the edge of Iowa City, by the airport, at the fringe of academic and middle-class life.

Our conversations are our nurture and our challenge. We share more deeply. Our stories of accomplishment: hers — as an experienced biologist and how she went about developing her intuitive skills; mine — as a first-class Girl Scout, possibly the longest matriculating Palmer student to survive and graduate and of pitching a no-hitter, thanks to my adroit and agile team, in Iowa's AAA State Softball Tournament. We share our devastations: hers — when her major oceanography professor makes her PhD contingent upon fucking him and, when she refuses, she has to quit the program as he gives all her hard-collected data to the woman who will soon became his wife; mine — having to reject the hell-fire threats of my early Lutheran pastor (I dared the lightning to strike, which it didn't), then losing the fragile family unity we barely had to Mom ending her life in the hopelessness of her marriage and that same church.

Our paths have taught us to trust the inherent healing capacities of people, animals and the world. Although we have differing approaches and do not state it as such quite yet, we essentially believe that Love heals all, which might be viewed as the nature of our religion. Occasionally we descend into behaving like our fathers — me cutting and critical; she angry and punishing.

On the more usual lighter note, if our conversation generates a particular sequence of words, it often triggers a 1950s or sixties musical engram. We might just sing a few lines — maybe from the Fifth Dimension, *The*

Wizard of Oz or even Meg Christian in love with her gym teacher. "She was a big strong woman…"

But, today I am driving this old black Dodge van given to us by my dad who, after mother's death, rapidly remarried and now lives just outside of Davenport. It became usable as soon as we replaced the front wheel bearings. The windows are wide open, our bare arms slouch on the side doors, our short haircuts wave and snap in the humid breezes. We are driving away from the Hilton because Karen has spent an hour on the phone talking to an old geezer named Chester L Miller, with just an L for a middle name. From my side, I hear, "Mmhmmm. Mmhmmm. Mmhmmm. Hmm Yeah. Unh hunh."

He has convinced us to rent his asbestos-sided one-story house with a garage at its back alley down in Wellman, population 1,400. We can take the university vanpool up to our university jobs. I imagine I'd rather take a commuter train to and from a stone cottage in a little town with stables, two coffee houses, a small organic grocery and a pub. But I'm not going to think of that now.

The van tires rhythmically tap along. We are engulfed by the corn sea.

We are not in some reverie of how things should be. This isn't the venture of a couple of twenty-year-olds. No, we're post-WWII baby boomers, products of the age of nuclear anxiety. Pre-Oprah.

We each have had our own *come to chiropractic* experiences — mine the repercussions of running my bicycle into a parked car and ripping my left sacroiliac joint when I was ten; Karen's from migraine headaches when she worked for the forest service, seeking medical help which failed, then, on the recommendation of a friend, getting treatment from a chiropractor. The headaches never returned.

Treeless green streams past the window. The single-point perspective of cornrows going to infinity draws the eye down into dark fleeting fissures.

Karen reclines attentively in the passenger seat in khaki shorts and a red-and-white-checked shirt. Her slim, smooth legs stretch out above the glove box while Paws the cat, lounges on her lap. Paws is a one-eyed, brown-and-black-striped tabby with polydactyl toes on her front feet. She is native to a rough neighborhood in Davenport student housing where she had some accident that blinded her right eye. Every couple months, if that eye gets cloudy or runny, I adjust her neck with a light rotary break move that a friend taught me and it clears right up.

We are at this place in our lives because we each chose to take up chiropractic as a profession — a profession that doesn't come with anything like a safety net for your double back flip in pike position daring. But, as of now, it seems we have solved the quest for the least expensive house in two contiguous counties. That's where we're headed. It just requires that we clean up someone else's shitpile and listen to the yarns of old Chester Miller. We can do that.

The tires tap on the two-lane road as the Magic Bubble of Iowa City fades away. It certainly beats a California commute.

This is an unfamiliar journey for us. But even in Reagan's America, professional middle-class white women must do what we must to make an independent living. Even in a profession where people and other health professionals, who know us not at all and who know little of what we do, feel free to express their adamant opinions.

It's thirty-five miles with one swooping curve south, then a right-hand turn west at the four-way stop and a final six bucolic miles through the English River Valley. We're here! We pass Wellman's golf course with its ecologically correct, but mostly old-fashioned, sand greens; then Casey's General Store for gas, pizza, and donuts; then the imposing limestone Methodist church. In two more blocks we would pass the skating rink and the huge corn storage bins out west of town. Instead, we turn left on the little state road south toward the old railroad tracks and Smith Creek at the southern part of town.

It is curious to wonder why we've landed in this place. It's not something we know yet — probably some karmic, astrological, DNA-fulfillment sort of reason that we are unsure of since we are simply making the best of our finances at the moment. Our place is just here on the right in this neighborhood of handsome trees and fifty-to-one-hundred-year-old homes.

Simultaneous personal problems, work problems and physical symptoms may have a common dysfunctional belief underneath it all.

Chester's House

There's no parking on the state highway in front of our little rental house so we turn at the cross street to get to the alley behind. The van bumps onto the ancient driveway of the old garage. We take our first proprietary look at the long narrow yard. Paws shakes her forepaws in the lush grass and has her first sniffs of small town.

KAREN: *Chester was saying this is likely where the drugs got exchanged. We'll definitely be sprucing up the neighborhood.*

MARGARET: *It's what we used to say in the Girl Scouts: Leave your campsite better than you found it. Remember that Texas mayor saying, "We got to get us some of those gays, since they take such good care of their neighborhoods."*

Oh! This is gagging me," says Karen, pulling one end of stinky carpet off the tiny room's floor. It leaves black pocks of rug tissue attached to the planks beneath. "If we didn't need to use this room, we should just close it off. Phew."

We gather up pungent newspapers and the smelly rugs. We're cleaning up after unruly cats and undiapered babies — a lifestyle that neither of us is familiar with. Our T-shirts are sticky; there are smudges at our nipples. She's got her short blonde hair wrapped up in a turquoise bandanna and I'm wearing a faded cotton ball cap. I take a clean tissue from my shorts pocket and wipe a particularly greasy blob off her biceps brachii. She looks at me with a steady smile. "Oh well, honey," she says. "It's affordable, and until we know where we're going, it's the price we pay for our independence."

"I know, babe. And this will be a warm cozy bedroom." I wag my tongue across my upper lip and grin at our filthiness. "And private."

I carry the final bags of detritus, a box of papers and a destroyed mop head through the kitchen and out its back door through a curious rectangular storage room with twelve-inch planks on the walls. I maneuver through a similar plank door onto a cement slab on the sun side near some recently bloomed lilac bushes. I turn right and portage through the lush grass of the backyard to dump this crap in the trashcan. There's another house back here, across the alley. It's Mennonite spick-and-span with a well-kept glassed-in porch. Perhaps someone watches from the fastidious depths.

I meet up with Karen in the tiny little bathroom just beyond the kitchen. The grubby little sink is now pleasurably white. A clamp-on shade softens the bare bulb over the medicine cabinet. The bulb connects to the wall socket by one of Chester's innovative little-white-wire solutions. We wash up using Tom's liquid soap. "Let's go into our empty living room and have some lunch," I say. "Here's another bandanna to dry your hands and face. We've got egg salad with Romaine, Vidalia onion and black olives."

The front door is propped open facing Ninth Avenue. Karen stretches her legs out, her back against the wall with a bowl of the lunch and I join her with a sandwich crammed full of lettuce. Ninth Avenue, the state highway, continues south to a T-intersection. A left turn east goes toward Washington, the county seat, and right goes west toward Sigourney and Fairfield. We can't know yet that one day we will have patients from all these little towns.

It looks like the trailer to the Hitchcock movie *North by Northwest* out there. I suppose it is. It is on this road that we will watch surprising vehicles pass by, like the old yellow school bus full of weanling piggies, their little pale snouts wiggling above the rear glass safety door. Or the stacked wire pens of turkeys, feathers blowing all directions in the wind, getting hauled to their next housing or to their final plastic shroud, before becoming dinner.

Muscle testing bypasses conscious, rational thought allowing the Body to reveal its stored experience and memory.

Welcome to Wellman

Our conversation continues in the front room of the newly cleaned rental house.

MARGARET: *Remember that X-ray from the Palmer Collection of the farm kid who had a flying nail pierce his neck?... Embedded itself right along the posterior arch of his atlas? ... Discovered years later in X-rays to determine his atlas listing for an upper cervical adjustment?*

KAREN: *Yes. What a story! And I remember my field doctor, old Russ Miller's upper cervical adjustments. Instead of having me lie on a side posture table like we learned, he'd have me sit up and then stabilize my head while I was sitting with my ear in a sort of baseball-mitt contraption on the wall. Then he'd do his toggle wrist thrust on my atlas. Startling at first but with a great sensation after... like my brain flushed and cleared out."*

MARGARET: *I remember having X-rays taken for other students' requirements. The first time was when I was twenty-two. The results shocked me. "This is the spine of a thirty-year-old with osteophytes and signs of aging." Wow! I had a second set taken just a couple years ago, in my mid thirties ... after ten years of organic food and no more cigarettes. Guess what it said? "This could be the spine of a twenty-year-old. The vertebrae have smooth borders with few osteoarthritic changes." I loved discovering that bones are not immutable rocks.*

After lunch, lying with my smudged bare legs stretched up the wall in postprandial relaxation, I ask Karen if she's going to miss Seattle and the ocean.

"Well I'm beginning to think of these lazy undulating hills as land waves," she says. "They're awfully quiet though, without the ocean's roar."

"That's because we don't yet know the sound of an ocean of corn growing."

She pulls off the bandanna covering her hair and wipes her hands, ignoring my reply. "I've had it with big insurance practices," she says. "But, I'm glad I took that time as the intake doc for such a big practice — examining the new patients, then taking their full spine X-rays. I was told to circle something on each X-ray picture in the area of the patient's chief complaint."

A bird twitters from the neighbor's nonrotating lawn windmill out the double windows. There's the scent of Murphy's Oil Soap in the air.

"In nine months of examining and X-raying people all day, I saw S-curves, hump curves, swaybacks and an acre of osteoarthritic white patches. But guess what? When I rechecked them in six weeks for their insurance re-exam, almost everybody, no matter what their chief complaint, had improved — even if their X-ray was much the same. During that time there were only three people with some kind of textbook pathology. So it makes me feel fine about using muscle testing and not taking X-rays. If I suspect fracture or cancer, I'll refer them out. You examine that many people in the flesh, then see their spines on the film, it gives you an intuition about them."

Our elbows intertwine; she has her back against the wall next to my upstretched legs. It's small-town, Sunday-afternoon quiet. The sun is still quite high. The little front lawn is softened by our big shade trees.

I guess we should muster. "OK, babe, enough chiropractic nostalgia; we've got to get our stuff down here." Our dirty arms squeeze, then release. I bend my knees and swing on to my side. Upright, I reach out and give her a tug to her feet.

A week and three van trips later we're in the living room again, unpacking books and boxes and arranging my curb-rescued sofa and chairs. I see a woman walk from the alley past the two sets of double windows, coming around toward our front door. She has graying dark hair stretched back under her little white mesh cereal-bowl-shaped head covering. Mrs. Mennonite Woman has come knocking. Her natural demeanor seems sober and stern, but she brightens and seems happy to meet us. Hardworking hands offer a warm, tangy-smelling rhubarb pie — probably from the pie bush back near the alley. "I have no need to come in," she says. "I just want you to know it's nice to have you in the neighborhood." I step out under the porch overhang, with its little wooden filigree designs and rotting ornamental posts, just for a minute to thank her, while holding the fragrant crust with shiny plops of pink sauce. Her name is Mrs. Schlabaugh and she's lived across the back alley for fifty-five years.

About two hours later, we're debating which books go on the front-room bookshelf and the neighbor next door to our north, Mrs. Harold Greene, from the yellow house with the smiling green trim, drops by to say how she and her husband think it's great that we are here. We have another threshold conversation and discover that they have three daughters, one of whom is the town clerk, married to the son of a former mayor. This woman is tall, with an old-man-like face. She smiles shyly as she easily offers a zucchini bread loaf and a jar of apple butter, as though she does this daily. I guess that might be possible.

Later still, while rearranging dishes and my varied spice containers — little juice jars and tiny brown India soda bottles with cork tops for ginger, peppercorns, cayenne peppers, turmeric, cardamom and a marmite jar for the ground cloves — in the really tall cupboards that go up to the nine-foot-high ceiling, comes another knock at the front door. I walk the length of the house to open it once more, this time to a chest-high basket bursting with unrecognizable objects and pamphlets and a jolly voice announcing, "Welcome Wagon!"

Then I see a head behind the basket, big-lens glasses and bottled-port-wine-colored hair. Here's another older woman, this one a twinkling extrovert offering us a sampling of the community fare. She steps in, clearly wanting to check us out. "I live next door," she says as the basket nods toward the beige-sided house with few windows and the non-rotating lawn windmill that we see when we go out our side porch.

"I'm Eunice Bontrager, I've lived here several years now since my husband passed. I am the local Welcome Wagon greeter and Amway representative and member of the Asbury Methodist church. We're having a potluck next weekend. That is, the church is. You know it's the big church up on the highway, and Lindy Evans and I would like to invite you to come. Lindy is an elementary school teacher in her thirties. We like to do things together."

She rushes right along still balancing the basket, "I've noticed that you two are cleaning up this house of Chester Miller's and that is so good because I think there were lots of drug deals happening in this house and in the alleyway behind."

The basket sways emphatically from side to side. "That alley starts at the side of my house and curves around behind us and I saw more vehicles pass by than I thought quite normal when that young woman was living here with her child."

And cats, I think, finishing her lengthy preamble in my head. "Can I take that? Would you like a cup of coffee or tea?" I say aloud, mentally wondering about the state of our cups and supplies and what one says in such a moment.

"Oh that's OK, but yes you can." The basket teeters as her big lenses peer past me into the room to see what she can see. "I just wanted to drop this off for you. And officially meet you … both." She leans in, scans for Karen who has abruptly faded into hiding. She offloads the unruly basket into my arms.

It is my turn to speak from the basket. "Well I'm Margaret and this is Karen … Well you'll meet her … "

She finishes my sentence. "At the church potluck I hope. Why don't we plan to come by for you and we can all walk up the street together? Next Sunday? A week from today? Let's say five-thirty?"

With that she turns and I see her dark skirt, pastel-blue blouse and stalwart black shoes stride toward the street, her now-empty hands marching at her sides. I am holding this basket of invitations from the small town businesses, the Wellman-Scofield Public Library, the Chat and Chew, several church pamphlets, a mug from an insurance company, some apples, magnets from the Chevy dealer and two key chains from the Ford dealer plus samples of Amway detergent and dish soap.

Ah, the essence of Wellman is in my hands.

When dialoguing with the subconscious, the person makes a statement like I am who I want to be in my Life *or* I am who I want to be in my relationship. *Then we muscle test to reveal what the Body has come to believe.*

Potluck Panic

We're in the kitchen. The white wooden cabinets that reach the nine-foot ceiling seem tall and out of reach.

MARGARET: *I don't have much experience with potlucks.*

KAREN: *It can't be that hard, can it?*

MARGARET: *I'm sure it's not for a practiced wife or mother who whips out cookies or casseroles on demand.*

KAREN: *When I used to go to potlucks with my grandmother, I had to follow behind and only take from the kitchens she knew to be clean or she would glare at me.*

All week I stew about what to make for the upcoming potluck. I review my scant past contributions. Once I experimented and made an olive oil mayonnaise and took it to a staff potluck when I worked at Mercy Hospital as an inhalation therapist. It was delicious, but lost without the potatoes, eggs, onions and spices. Every Sunday night for a year at Palmer I took a quart of Häagen Dazs over to a friend's house to watch PBS Masterpiece Theatre. And yes, I have invited people to my house and made lasagna or quiche or broccoli soup, but with a new strange kitchen and the small town time warp I want something less dear.

None of these experiences are particularly helpful, faced with my impending deadline. I feel like this is not something that can be settled with a bag of chips. Karen does not bother with such worries and feels no crisis or peer pressure, particularly in the cooking department. Her worries come in the cleaning department.

After work on Wednesday evening I sit down with my ancient *Joy of Cooking* and plunge into the pages, an idea-starved person. The index, like the exacting recipe instructions, is a joy to read, however, there is no category for potluck. There is pot liquor, pot pie, pot roast ... and then, potato. There's nearly a column and a half of potato recipes. I think, *How about scalloped potatoes?*

Sunday evening I carry Karen's red enamel pot filled with baked-on crustiness and soft rich potatoes up the street with Eunice, Lindy and Karen to the Methodist church basement with its caramel paneling and chocolate-colored tiles. I feel like we are just moving along in a conveyor-belt sort of way. Smiling, nodding, greeting full-faced, wrinkly, beaming faces near a huge table of food. Jellos; unidentifiable casseroles; finger sausages; brownies; red, yellow, and purple pies; and now scalloped potatoes. OK, this is going to be fine.

I place my pot and hide the lid in an accessible place. I turn to join our group and find Eunice introducing us to the Methodist minister. I smile and put out my hand toward a blonde-headed, bland-faced man in his clerical collar and black shirt. A pause. As we each fully look at the other, our hands nearly clasping, my mind leaps to an uninvited memory of seeing him in a gay club up in Iowa City a couple years ago.

His demeanor rather freezes just as our hands meet. I forget that this is a potluck and, therefore, somewhat my party and I miss the opportunity to save the moment. Being the new person in my first outed outing, I just wish for a wink and a smile so I can relax, not blow his cover, if that's what's required, and enjoy the church basement. Our smiles have warped a bit, and he retracts his Methodistness slightly. He turns back to Eunice, then begins edging away. I look to see who might have noticed this not-so-welcoming welcome. Karen briefly looks up from checking out pie, possibly feeling the passing shadow.

An hour later we have met several upright members of the Methodist flock, heard about grown children, husbands' recoveries, quilting and eaten our fill of the "luck." I gather the potato pot, which has two servings remaining and move the group toward fresh air. Back down Ninth Avenue at our new home we say thanks and goodnight to our tour guides. We step inside and fall into our chairs without words. After a bit, Karen says, "Potatoes were good."

Muscle testing is a binary thing — the muscle being tested either holds strong or gives way, revealing the Body's message.

Here Comes Chester

MARGARET: *Remember when I tried for that test-editing job up in the City? Or up to the City, as they say here. So I wouldn't have to label samples in the pathology lab? My work experience included two years writing copy and editing book covers at Sunstone Press, plus two years proofing at the NM Legislature; just no master's degree in English...*

KAREN: *And then after refusing to hire you, they call and ask if they can use your work experience sheet as an example for their employees.*

MARGARET: *At least they called for permission. And I got to tell them it had never gotten me a job.*

KAREN: *Oh well, we're getting by with our lab jobs, thanks to Chester's little piece of heaven here.*

I sit in a foldable lawn chair behind the house. Not my usual habit... sitting. Today I'm just waiting for Chester to come by. There's no need to rush about this afternoon. In this new place we're each in a time of reflection, awaiting the opportunity to take our Iowa State Boards. I'm ready to burst into a new dimension as I take weekend trips to Iowa City, Fairfield and Chicago with a group of local therapists pursuing this new subject of Educational Kinesiology. It just happens to be a perfect fit with what I've already learned.

I stretch my legs out and let my sacrum rest on the front of the chair to momentarily relieve my gluteal muscles from the sinking webbing. My neck tilts back at the top of the chair. From this vantage, in the small-town afternoon quiet, I see the sun just fringing the tops of Mrs. Mennonite Woman's tallest trees across the alley.

This is a terribly slouched posture in which to contemplate the evolution of kinesiology — historically the academic study of body movement. For example, what is the effect of this ridiculous chair on my spinal integrity or my muscle strength? If someone tested my outstretched arm in my compromised position, by pressing on it, it's likely to be weak because of suboptimal electrical nerve signal to my arm muscle.

Distractedly, I stretch further and glance at Chester's old two-story garage to my right or, as he would say squinting through his cloudy lenses, "Just there to the north." What I see are aging gray shingles for siding and a rusting metal roof. This disguises all the hardwood planks and frame members that make up the two stories and roof of this tough little building. Through the plank door there's a small window and workbench on the near wall; a block and tackle over a beam on the far side; and a waist-high pile of hickory, oak and walnut boards stacked on the upper floor. Clearly, this all comes from a time of accomplished carpentry and abundant wood. I begin to see the reward of Wood Choppin' Chester's arduous life.

Thinking of that pile of hardwood gives me a melancholy feeling of abundance and reminds me, didn't he say he'd be right over? I guess it's fine to relax and wait when the grass is lush, the breeze is a delicate whisper and the puzzle of light coming through the trees is gauzy soft.

In practice, many puzzles are elucidated by muscle testing, which is used in Applied Kinesiology. An internal salvo of electrical discharge is translated into a simple strong or not-strong muscle response. Choose the muscle — outstretched arm, opposing finger and thumb, raised knee — one that stays strong and unwavering when it's pushed on. Then provide a single challenge to the system and push. Does the muscle stay strong or give way? A challenge would be like pressing on a misaligned vertebra or putting a supplement under the tongue or even making a statement to see if the body supports it or not. It's important to only ask one question at a time. But, with careful application, a very complex internal response is transformed into binary action. Seems harder to describe than to experience.

I look up from my reverie as a faded old Chevy sedan rocks to a halt by the rhubarb pie bush in the alley. I sit tall in my chair now and come back from my ruminations. Here's Chester L Miller. He's sort of avoided around town because of his endless conversationalism. I've already seen people turn around or change course on the street to escape him. He is a short, stout, full-faced seventy-five-year-old man with ruined knees who has probably cut down more original Iowa trees than I've seen in my lifetime — thus the garage and a woodpile taller than his other two-story house. He is our unlikely landlord. On weekends, he often clambers out from his worn front seat to limp across the lawn, bringing us some delicacy from his 1930s kitchen.

"You 'ens want some tapiocky?" He beams. "And I brought pickled eggs in beet juice." Other times it's creamy yellow potato salad, from just-dug potatoes and onions, or perhaps a sweating jar of frothy purple grape juice from his ancient, tangled vine. His garden is the last of its kind in this fading farm town. With carrots and kohlrabies and trellises of peas and tomatoes, to me it's a completely foreign, teeming, abundant universe.

Having made his offering, he falls into the other webbed lawn chair arranging his legs and getting as comfortable as he can. His blue overalls and frayed T-shirt confidently arranged, he sets to talking.

He's not the curious type so he asks no questions and is not interested in what I'm thinking about. It's just as well because if he asked about normal things, like family or heritage, the story would be short and unflavorful since, in my family we are all distant, with meager communication. I prefer to listen while he talks about what's coming along in the garden.

He journeys from the garden to what he made for supper and then on to how he ruined those knees jumping out of a pickup truck. I think about that and know they are most likely worn and shredded, having long ago missed the opportunity to heal well. And he goes on about his stepson, the junior banker, how proud he is, then about having to drive sixty miles to Cedar Rapids on the interstate and his plan to be safe by driving fifty miles per hour in the left hand passing lane.

He moves on to the war, about losing his front teeth to backfire in a machine gun nest, about felling trees and winning wood-chopping contests, swelling with pride and bragging about his younger physique. Then on to farming and tending piglets and how an old sow makes the best sausage.

The sun is considerably lower now, creating filigree in the trees. The stories begin to repeat and my sitter is numb. I say, "Well, Chester, I've got to get a few more things done."

"Yes," he says grinning, "I know I talk too much." He launches into another story. I stand and repeat myself. He hoists himself out of his chair, arranges his lower legs and feet beneath his knees and shambles back to his car.

Karen doesn't participate in these conversations. She had grandparents who lived on a farm. But for me, with no grandparents and growing up in 1950s tract housing where they bulldozed all the topsoil, listening to an old geezer who smells of earth and sweat is something radical.

When a muscle is being tested, it's an odd sensation to think you are holding strong, then feel your muscle give way. Often people will say, "You pushed harder," because it feels like it when, in fact, the circuit is just "browned out."

Probing the Universe

MARGARET: *That guy you work with sounds like a real arrogant, misguided ...*

KAREN: *Undereducated, incompetent, mean fundamentalist? ... Yes.*

MARGARET: *And insecure and promoted beyond his capability. At least he doesn't know that you are ... what is it they say about gay people?*

KAREN: *An abomination against God, of course.*

People who've been around Iowa City for a while know that Highway 1 sidles up from the south, takes a smooth, arcing curve to the east, ambles into the morning sun, then slides over a gentle hillside and there's the Iowa Cityscape. Today I'm heading to the far east side of the City so I pass old Dane's Dairy Road and the iconic Paul's Farm Store that we refer to as "Paul's of Iowa," turn left onto Riverside Drive and head straight for the university's spread — my undergraduate alma mater. I turn right at the Burlington Street Bridge and cross the tomboyish Iowa River.

The river slips through the city after a graceful meander along curvaceous "beautiful land" (what the brochures say is the meaning of "Iowa") hillsides, yet resolves to toughen up as she swallows a glut of agricultural wastes and biocide chemicals, then further prepares her gullet to carry any pharmaceuticals from university hospitals like antibiotics, antipsychotics, blood thinners, statins and immunosuppressants that have eluded the sewage treatment plant. Even so, she's a celebrated beauty, admired from both the east and west sides of the university campus.

Highway 1 continues up the hill and skirts round the ever-evolving downtown, on out past the last neighborhood bar and the old Sinclair station with its benevolent little green dinosaur looking around as if to say *Where am I? How did I get here? Am I related to the fossils who became these fuels?* Just before Interstate 80 and points north is the bright orange roof of the old Howard Johnson's Motel. This is the destination for today's class — Introduction to Educational Kinesiology.

I park and enter, following signs to a room with three good-sized windows, somewhat compensating for the dreaded fluorescent lights. About twenty HoJo orange plastic chairs are arranged in a spacious circle. There's no back of the room to sequester oneself, just immediate total immersion. I put a plain-paged notebook and pen on a chair, then step back a bit to survey the territory.

"Oh, hi," says the woman with big glasses whom I back into.

"Oops, sorry. I don't really like to sit until the last minute."

Then, immediately, it is the last minute. I move my notebook to my lap and take my seat. Our two women teachers have organized their handouts and matching orange Brain Gym® booklets on a table by a window and taken chairs in the circle. One has curly dark hair trimmed to just above her shoulders. She has a wide smile, caramel-colored eyes and beautiful dark caterpillar eyebrows. The taller of the two has light hair and gray eyes. Her hair splits over her athletic shoulders to the level of her scapulae.

Then comes the friendly "We're in this together" opening, unfamiliar to me because in professional school the didact preaches from the front of the room. Introductions all round — including each of us. The teachers are from Fairfield, south of Wellman, home of Maharishi Mahesh Yogi's Institute of Management and his meditation empire. They studied with Dr. Brain Gym® himself, Paul Dennison, Education PhD, and his wife, Gail.

Now we, the class, must go around the circle: What is our name? What do we do? What do we want to get out of the class? To me that last question is like a store clerk who asks, "Did you find everything?" And I think *Well, hmm. Everything? Actually no ... I'm also looking for a time expander and world peace.* I'm only this literal when I'm a little nervous and it makes me snarky. But how can I know what to want? I don't know what they are teaching.

There's a smiling therapist with a nasally, breathy voice who wants to help her clients; a short, sturdy seamstress who likes the idea of "switched on learning;" and several grade school teachers, including the woman with the big glasses, who want to help their students' reading and comprehension. They all clearly know more about what we're going to learn than I do.

Then it's my turn. "I am looking forward to learning more about these integrative learning methods...and I guess, achieving world peace." The room happily quiets.

The teaching team begins. They trade off introducing subjects, demonstrating and moving us around. This is a day of participation learning. We are going to use muscle testing for before and after assessments — an outstretched arm testing weak beforehand and hopefully strong after doing the integrative movement.

To be sure that the person being tested is not neurologically disorganized or "switched," which would give false answers, we learn to connect the end points of front and back meridian pathways. Touch pubic bone and just below the lower lip; look down and ground to Earth. Touch sacrum and just above the upper lip and connect with Sky. Massage vigorously under collarbones next to sternum. I like to call it quality control, just like they do in the laboratory.

We learn several Brain Gyms® — movements designed to connect the left and right brains and to improve verbal comprehension. This is a cute name for hand/eye movements using "lazy eights," which are big swooping infinity symbols — ∞ — that we draw in the air or on a chalkboard, while our eyes follow our hands or the chalk. This is thought to turn on areas of the brain and to activate the major pathway between the hemispheres. We uncurl our ears and stretch our calves for brain stimulation. At other times, we make exaggerated cross-crawl movements with outstretched arms and legs. The various exercises are designed to help anyone, but especially children, to read, listen, articulate and write with comprehension. Communicating pathways in the brain can freeze up under stress, like test anxiety or speaking in public.

My partner is the therapist. We draw swooping infinity shapes in the air with our thumbs and follow with our eyes to globally activate our brains and do cross crawls to integrate thinking. I consider the similarities of these movements with this new therapy called EMDR (Eye Movement Desensitization and Reprocessing), which changes emotional focus and allows the Body to put things in the past instead of continuing to be a distracting force in current time.

Bringing our outstretched arms together and interlacing our fingers at our foreheads creates a metaphorical brain hemisphere connection. These are simple patterned movements to activate connections in the neural network. It helps to remember that the right brain hemisphere controls the left side of the body and processes global understanding; while the left hemisphere controls the right side and processes linear transactional thinking. Over time, I will find these simplest of activities are capable of initiating profound change as part of a much deeper Emotional Balance.

The marvelous thing is that these integrative movements and hand/eye concepts are waaaaay simple, because they re-educate the body at a fundamental level of organization. I guess that's why it's called Educational Kinesiology.

Simultaneously, the disturbing thing is that these integrative movements and hand/eye concepts are waaay simple. I can just imagine that left-brained adults will find it easy to scoff because we are just doing brain reorganization and not brain surgery or prescribing medications. It's not some expensive thingamabob-ism with an unpronounceable name that must therefore be important and effective. At the moment we don't have EEG recordings or brain imagery to give us the full authority that those data give. Instead we have affect change, mood change, a taller posture, a calmer demeanor and those things that unaccountably change in the outside world. Damn these subjective results. They may make you feel better, but where does it show on the chart?

At the end of the day we hug our teachers. Unheard of, but it fits as a celebration of accomplishment. I may not be used to it, but it seems good for me to surrender. I return home rather pleased that the events of the day weren't really like learning — more like letting out the seams of the garment of my current knowledge to expand into unexpectedly fascinating attire. I hope to fit into it.

Over the next few months Rhonda, the therapist from class, becomes a colleague. We join two other therapists from her office and the seamstress and then a guy who is an anatomy postdoc. Together we are a fledgling group but, because of our intense interest, the next three levels of class are offered in our area — Iowa City and Fairfield. These next levels expand beyond the left brain/right brain integration to a top/down centering concept and a front/back focusing concept. Pretty soon we are beyond improving reading and writing to something more like rewiring the subconscious using the Dennison's Seven Dimensions of Intelligence concept.

If something I study doesn't help me in some way, I don't trust it to help others. But at each juncture, in each new class, I find something improved about how I relate to others or I become more forgiving with myself. Then I take it out for a spin to try on my workmates and, of course, Karen.

"I want a Balance," she says on a Friday evening, after a terrible day at the State Hygienic Laboratory. "We are reduced to hiding glassware so we have some for our shift because Dillard is such a bad manager. Plus, he was leering at me this morning as I walked in and started in on some Christian witnessing thing completely inappropriate in the workplace. Morale is just getting worse and worse."

"OK. Let's do it. Let me get my notebook."

We do the clearing checks I learned and plunge in. We muscle test statements she makes about working in that atmosphere and how it makes her feel. She hates the personal attacks, but even more dislikes being treated unprofessionally. This seems obvious, but since we have no balancing domain over Dillard, she has to change herself to change the outcome. So, we tune her system to the statement, "My laboratory work is an esteemed professional endeavor." She does some cross crawls, taps a meridian and resets. Now she's strong for that statement.

After we finish, she says, "I feel calmer. Maybe I can relax this weekend."

And so we do, with chores, a dinner out on Saturday, a walk on Sunday. By Monday evening I've sort of forgotten about the Balance. Then Karen arrives home laughing and singing, "What a Wonderful World."

"Guess what? Guess what?" she says.

"Something good, it looks like. They fix the vents on the ether hood?"

"Not yet, but they found that the intake fresh air vent was right next to the exhaust vent with all those volatile chemicals, so they will...but this is even better!"

"Better than not being drugged at the end of the day? Do tell."

"Well, it could be...must be...in any case is synchronistically related to my Balance!"

"What? What? What?"

"Apparently Dillard came in over the weekend to do some cleaning out. He dumped samples from the freezers that hadn't been tested yet — important samples...some of which were chain-of-custody legal samples...and he was demoted! Instantly! He was removed from our lab and is now working in the basement with nothing at all to do with us! I don't have to deal with him anymore!"

"The basement — great place for a creepy guy! Wow. That's just … Wow!"

If a muscle tests strong for a statement, I must assume the subconscious believes it and it is the person's Truth even if it's completely irrational or paradoxical. In other words, I must let the Truth be True.

Moving Up the Hill

Fall 1987. Margaret is sprawled on a satiny blue bedspread in a Chicago hotel. At home, Karen sits on the floral couch with Paws on her lap, holding the blue handset, trailing the spiraling cord that spans the long living room from around the kitchen door jamb.

MARGARET: *Well, class is intense and fun.*

KAREN: *Are you learning anything?*

MARGARET: *Yes. About using meridian points to change emotional responses. But the most monumental thing happened at lunch break.*

KAREN: *You fed your sandwich to the pigeons?*

MARGARET: *No. Guess what! The Wilk versus AMA lawsuit was decided yesterday after all these years. I was doing my usual squat down to read the Chicago Tribune headlines in the paper machine. Listen to this!*

Judge Susan Getzendanner found the American Medical Association guilty of unlawful conspiracy in restraint of trade to contain and eliminate the chiropractic profession and issued a permanent injunction to prevent such future behavior.

Of course it came out on a Friday so it would be diluted in the Saturday papers. But, it was a thrill to read it here in Chicago at the scene of the drama!

One almost-fall morning we hear a short inviting *meow* from under the bedroom window. Paws jumps into the open window well. A subdued, groaning wail of authority follows. I pull on a shirt and peer into the barely lit grassy space between us and the neighbor's garage. It's a strawberry blonde cat. Maybe green eyes. Just sitting there politely.

It takes a few days of comings and goings before we all decide to enlarge our family with another striped cat, this one with sunny-tinged orange stripes. I root for naming her Rosie, short for Rosalind Franklin since I'm currently reading about her in *The Eighth Day of Creation*. She took the X-ray diffraction images that allowed Watson, Crick and Wilkins to surmise the repeating double helix structure of DNA and then win the Nobel Prize.

Upon further investigation, Karen says, "She's a boy." There goes my idea. Instead he becomes Butchie for his sexy swagger, and later that winter he joins Paws in the quilts bunched around Karen with a pile of textbooks on the couch as she prepares for her qualifying boards in Des Moines. The frigid wind is most cunning, shuddering the cold aluminum frames of the once sunlight-filled double windows, which are now close gray shrouds. I too am curled up with books like *The Mists of Avalon*, *The Eighth Day of Creation* and even *The White Goddess* — which enthralls me for as long as I look at the page, but when I look up, I can't recall anything I've just read.

Karen passes her oral board exams, successfully

recognizing a newly fractured navicular bone at the base of the thumb and presenting a stellar assessment and case review. Immediately, a major shift occurs in town. Jack Ross, older of the two town chiropractors, dies of a massive, crushing heart attack on a dark, frozen January night. Knowing that this town of 1,400 people has always supported two chiropractors, Karen sits up abruptly, disturbing the cats, and proclaims that we should open a home practice here! "Just think," she says, "No one knows us here. That's a plus. If we fail, no one will care."

I'm OK with the idea but have grown hesitant, with no inspiration or aspiration to offer.

"You're not sure you even want to practice now after enduring all those years in school?" She is incredulous with me. "It's all we know how to do. All we're fit for, even with no real experience."

"I know, I know," I say. "I just ... but ... well, let's check it out."

As spring comes around, there is one ad for a house to rent in *The Wellman Advance*. It's at the corner of Main on Seventh Street, one block up from Highway 22, which slices the town approximately in half. We stand on the sidewalk gazing up at the landlord-green, two-story, one-hundred-year-old house.

"Well, I don't think ..." I begin, as Karen says, "This will be perfect!"

We take an afternoon out of town and drive the countryside to get the perspective of what's around us. Clouds float low over the vast green fields. We land in Iowa City for coffee at The Great Midwestern Ice Cream Company. Sitting in the front window with chocolate almond and "pigs in the mud" (raspberries in chocolate) ice cream we watch clouds descend and darken the street. "I have to stop at the public library," I say as we finish up.

Crossing Washington Avenue, big splatting raindrops hit the pavement. "Let's hurry." We rush through the ped mall and down to the library before water begins gushing all around. Once inside, I say, "I'm going to mysteries and esoteric stuff."

"What are you getting there?"

"Today it's handwriting analysis."

"OK you go there first, and I'll meet you in mysteries."

I find her between the stacks of the whodunits, amidst the smells of inked pages of adventure and conviction that mysteries inspire. She's getting *D Is for Deadbeat* and Tony Hillerman's *Skinwalkers*. I add *Presumed Innocent* by Scott Turow and check us out with my Wellman-Scofield Public Library card, thanks to the honoring of cards from neighboring county libraries. Our little library is great for kids and I've found the entire Dorothy L. Sayers mystery collection there.

We head to the front door and find that the downpour has finished. The street is steamy wet while the air smells rested and new. We stop at the front entrance in the freshness. Just then the sun emerges from behind our heads and two arcs of rainbow embrace the eastern sky before us.

"There's a good omen for our new venture," says Karen.

"I know. The second is nearly as strong as the first."

"Well, let's do it."

We negotiate a two-year lease with intent to buy, assuming the venture doesn't go bust, from the owners, a Shiloh couple with two teenage daughters. The house has a certain dignity as it graces the gentle hill seven blocks up from Smith Creek at the southern border of town and four from the remaining storefronts of the downtown. We are across the street and up a block from the limestone Asbury Methodist Church edifice and its insistent morning, midday and evening bells. And of course we've met the blonde not-exactly-who–he-seems pastor.

We paint the house white, with a country-blue front door. We spruce up the little front porch and its wrought iron railings. I think the diamond window above the porch, with Paws sleeping on the sill, adds style.

Karen is going to cut her work at the hygienic lab to two days a week. She'll keep clinic hours on Monday, Wednesday and Friday. I have the sawyer at the lumberyard cut a beautiful crescent curve in the top of a smooth rectangle of good plywood. I paint it shiny white with a beautiful blue tree of life at the top. In glossy black, I letter CHIROPRACTICE along the top arch. And below the tree: Karen S. Zakar, D.C., Margaret J. Hansen, D.C., 646-6533 MWF 9-noon, 2-7.

We'll screw the sign onto the wooden siding next to the front door, just high enough that you can see it above the porch railing. We have a simple consistent plan. Keep to the hours, busy or not. Keep the house clean and vacuumed every morning. Keep the waste-baskets emptied at the end of each day. Then people can see that we are not scary lesbians — just conscientious, middle-aged doctors.

Nothing about a subconscious belief has to be rational, especially if it's a protective adaptation to a sick or abusive environment.

Two Patriarchs and a Hog

KAREN: *I know you said you'd be working on all of this, but you're going so slowly.*

MARGARET: *I know I have this need to get it all right. Want to help with sanding the hallway so we can get it stained? And we need to get these curtains sewed.*

KAREN: *I wish we could afford some nicer furniture. But at least I got that beautiful ceramic lamp from Kay of the Frogtown Potters for the adjusting room.*

MARGARET: *The furniture will be fine. People who come are focused on their pain. And that lamp makes the room. No one will even care that it's sitting on a painted table from the Goodwill.*

We're working away to be ready for patients. The big farm kitchen at the back is our only personal space downstairs. To keep us cheerful on gray days we've painted one wall a vibrant, wild blue and above the cupboards a strip of Western sunset orange. The middle room, which used to be a parlor, now has curtains we've made from soft, blue-print cotton for the three tall windows.

Karen's adjusting room is the snug little bedroom off this center room, with blue carpeting and light-blue patterned wallpaper. The front room is full of light from a large street-facing window and a double hung east window. We've found some inexpensive furniture with bumbly beige upholstery and now call this the waiting room.

Along the way, we have two run-ins with town patriarchs. The first when Karen takes a one-page business plan down to the Wellman Savings Bank.

As she tells of her encounter with the bank president, I imagine the scene. He in L.L.Bean khaki chinos and a sport coat behind a large wooden desk, squinting through tortoiseshell glasses, with a distaste similar to what he likely felt a few months ago when the Supreme Court ruled that the Rotary had to admit women.

Karen, wearing a crisp cotton shirt, has laid out her plan for beginning practice and requests $1,000 for a simple no-frills chiropractic table. Perhaps then, he smooths his balding, tanned head in feigned incredulity, before reciting reasons why that kind of investment is of no use to him or the bank. "With student loans like these, you should be a neurosurgeon," he says. At that great misconception and self-righteousness, she gets up from her chair and turns to leave. I imagine her color is up, her lips clamped in disgust. No doubt she is doing an internal eye roll at the all too familiar male superiority routine.

The second encounter involves the editor of the *Wellman Advance*. I write a little article introducing our home practice business and ourselves. It is my turn to visit their drab little office, just across the street and up from the bank. Copy in hand, I am thinking of a front-page article with a photo of us in front of the house and the gleaming new sign, similar to an article introducing a couple who have just opened a frame shop in one of the downtown storefronts with a front-page photo of them in their shop — a full article of introduction.

The newspaper's masthead proclaims, "The only newspaper that gives two whoops about Wellman IA." The old whooper himself is in the office. He is not a preppy dresser like the banker. He is mostly gray and saggy in the jowls, hair fringe, jacket and trousers … and attitude. "That's not possible," he grumbles. "We just can't do that sort of thing for everyone." I look around for the rush of everyone, then say, "We would like to introduce ourselves to the community. On the front page of next week's paper."

"We can do that, but it will cost you a $30 advertising fee. And we will have to label it an advertisement," he says with a certain satisfaction.

"OK. I will pay the fee, but would prefer you let it just be an article without the advertising label," I say, ditching the photo idea.

"I don't know about that," he says.

I wait. I wonder if he wants me to beg. The pause becomes quiet and serene. It is as though the walls are listening in rapt attention as a new adventure begins to unfold. The pause seems to swell and gather strength as it lengthens.

"Well, OK," he says.

"I'll write you a check now," I say, as though a fair business transaction has just occurred and not some petty quibbling. "That will be in next Thursday's paper. Correct?" Contriving for him to say something positive.

"Yes."

"Very good. Thank you." I leave the copy on the counter.

As I walk back up the hill, I let my memories run together. I think about how I could tell my Dad about these smug old men and he would side with me in a minute. That is, until he is talking to them, and then he'd reverse course.

I recall a hot languorous August afternoon at the Iowa State Fair. In the swine barn, amidst the heady livestock smells and buzz of flies, I remember peering into the pen of the largest boar champion. The old guy is benignly snoozing, surrounded by gaping onlookers, snout glistening, breaths coming in snorts of oblivion. Little dignified tusks poke through the tawny-pink flesh near his lip. His potholder-sized floppy ears twitch contentedly on the enormous thousand-pound body with its bristly hairs and delicate, droopy pink testicles as he grunts in his admirable maleness.

He's a picture of the contented non-ego-driven male — much more my type.

I begin to think that the conscious Mind would solve its problems if it could, but besides dreams and hypnosis, muscle testing seems like a great way to allow the conscious Mind to become aware of specifics of the subconscious Mind.

Doors Open

KAREN: *You know the practice-building advice always suggests getting to be part of your community by joining a church or service club.*

MARGARET: *Yes, you could always become a Rotary member with Gordon, the bank president.*

KAREN: *Or let's see, which church? The Methodists are still disallowing their gay clergy. We'd have to drive to someplace up in the City or Cedar Rapids, defeating the point of connecting with the community.*

MARGARET: *You need a group where you can talk about that newest book you're reading. Didn't I see Whitley Strieber's* Communion *on your nightstand?*

We are officially open ... Karen, that is to say, Dr. Karen has begun keeping clinic hours.

We are curious, yet nervous, kind of like it feels when inviting people to a party — excited, assured and hopeful, then on the actual day nonchalantly uncertain if anyone will show up. Each day I arrive home from the hospital lab wondering if anyone has come. I'm shocked to discover that she has sent away the first two patients. Then I learn the reasons.

The first potential patient is a tottering gray-haired lady in a dark shirtwaist dress and cardigan sweater, whom I've seen about town. Her middle-aged son helps her navigate the front steps. Within a few minutes of talk about the onset of her dizziness and the recitation of her list of prescription drugs, Karen tells her that she is most likely having a drug reaction which chiropractic adjusting won't help. She is sent back to her medical doctor for review.

The second is a local insurance guy. He has been a longtime patient of the other chiropractor in town and generally happy with his care. Karen is annoyed with him for his lack of loyalty and further does not want to steal her first patient. She questions why he is changing. "Well, he doesn't listen to me anymore," says the insurance guy.

"Are you talking with him?" she inquires.

"Well no, probably not."

"OK, return and talk to him. If you won't talk with him, you probably won't to talk with me."

Then on Friday afternoon as I return from work, I see a ten-year-old mostly white Chevy van parked out front. An obese man in a white, wrinkled dress shirt dozes in the driver's seat. I clap up the sturdy wooden steps of our now spick-and-span little porch and enter the foyer. A complicated conversation is coming from the front waiting room.

Men are speaking in formal, accented, authoritative voices. I glance through the double doors as I head up the stairs and see four or five Amish elders in their dark polyester pants, white shirts and suspenders, with lordly beards streaming from their lower jaws. I see the back of Karen's blonde head as she presides over the meeting. Halfway up the staircase, I overhear one of the Amish patriarchs ask her what church she goes to. Pausing incrementally mid-step to hear what she makes up, I hear her say, "Unitarian."

Then comes the retort, "That's not a church."

I disappear out of earshot. A grilling like that would silence me, but Karen's work-study/scholarship was to a small Presbyterian liberal arts college. She knows her Bible verses and brooks no religious arrogance. She'll do just fine as the interrogation continues.

Our little town is just a few fences over from the Amish community, which owns most of the still-organic acres around Kalona, six miles east of us. When someone leaves the Amish community and joins a less conservative church it is called jumping over the fence. As an outsider, I do not know the formalities of life in the Amish community. Except, that a nonAmish is an English. Among themselves, or when they don't want to include you in a conversation, they speak Pennsylvania Dutch — a simple German dialect.

The women wear polyester dresses, in bright greens, maroons and purples, with a bib-like front and gathered skirt held together with straight pins — no worldly buttons or zippers — like the men's trousers and shirts. A white cap "covers" long braided and wrapped hair, no wisps floating on a summer breeze, no bangs to shape a face. When the weather is cold, they wear a heavy, black wool cape-like coat and black bonnet with an upper parabolic curve squeezed around the cheeks and tied at the neck. In winter slush or in their barnyards, they wear zip-up rubber overshoes.

Amish women in our area tend to have strong, ample bodies. If two young women are sitting at a summer roadside stand selling sweet corn or other fresh produce, you will always see them sitting with their heads down, elbows in, reading something like a book of verse. I like to imagine them differently — in the fit bodies they must have: one girl lounging in a hammock, her arms crossed behind her head, softly humming; the other standing, leaning against the wooden wagon of produce, sleeves rolled up, head back sunning, while they wait to ably assist their customers with organic produce.

Strict Amish have rules that are not that clear to outsiders. For example, they cannot have telephones in their homes, but there is a phone in someone's barn for making appointments and doing farm business. They drive black covered buggies pulled by one or a pair of horses. Lighter carts are pulled by specially bred pacers. These are trim sleek animals with a gait that moves front and back legs of one side opposite the other at a smart handsome clip.

So the van outside the house is the transport for these men. It's OK to hire a ride in a rubber-tired vehicle if someone else drives (and pays for vehicle, insurance and gas), especially if the specific purpose involves going for health care. I even become aware of Amish who fly in airplanes to go to a faraway doctor. There is a little joke that asks, "How do you get an Amish to the moon?" Answer: "You put a chiropractor there."

Gasoline-powered tractors with metal-spiked wheels or plows pulled by great Belgian horses work their farm fields. At an Amish lumberyard, the saw is powered by a gas generator with long whirring belts, no electrical hookup. Complicated rules. The community gathers at someone's home on Sunday for services, so everyone bathes on Saturday. As many as forty black buggies can be seen in the driveways and along the roadside for a day of community. The only other time I see so many buggies gathered is at a land or implement auction. Then I will hear the story of an Amish farmer spending $250,000 cash for a farm for his children. I don't know if it's true, but if you don't pay into Social Security and Medicare, grow your own feed and food, are exceedingly thrifty and work your children and your family every minute of the day, well, I would think expenses would be minimal.

I still haven't learned who is behind country yard signs like "Do you hate sin?" which sends me into philosophical wonderment and annoyance. I only hate a few things, but I'm adding this question to that list. *Who are you to ask? Is this question about me? Do you hate me?* All the while I think, *And I'm just driving down a pastoral country road with unconcerned horses and goats in the fields minding my own business, and here you are in my business.*

After a time, I discover that if a person wants a less conservative group, they might jump over the fence to become Beachy Amish Mennonites. Maybe that's the name of the first patriarchal leader to move the faction to a less strict lifestyle — using electricity perhaps.

Then they might just jump another fence and become one of the versions of Mennonite. The preaching of the church is most likely quite conservative. Many of the women still cover their heads, but drive cars and have jobs. I have been passed on the highway by sedate sedans which Karen and I have come to call "Mennonite cars," driven by little beige or pastel persons wearing a head covering, yet speeding past.

The community looks out for its own, with exceptions for young women who get pregnant or are aggressed upon by lecherous male members and anyone who's gay and unwilling to live in a closet. In spite of supposedly being unworthy sinners, it seems the community defines making money as very pleasing in the sight of God.

Over the next fence would be Methodist, perhaps Lutheran. And now there's a new breed of charismatic fundamentalists, particularly among the younger generations. I have to wonder what fences we have hurdled as undefined, uncategorized, spiritual, possibly Buddhist-like, nearly-new-age healers.

I crack the upstairs door at the landing over the stairwell. Karen is now almost joking with them even as they remain in their puffed-up demeanor. "I'd be happy to care for you or your wives if you are willing to make an appointment," she says. "It's important to spend the time to get to the bottom of a problem. I believe you have a way to call, right?"

One says, "Doc Black will come down from the City to Elmer Yoder's place. We like him."

At the front door threshold Karen watches the backs of their hats and suspenders as they awaken their driver and climb into the van. I come down the steps as she says, "Well, they got their chance to check us out. Me too. Frankly I prefer men who bathe more often."

The point is to find out what's at work in the subconscious background — since it runs the show and may reveal itself in unwanted reactions, emotions or behaviors.

Shiloh

MARGARET: *OK, my mother was a Dorothy and she could be short with shopkeepers, but she would never have been so rude to a neighbor... not that she had any neighbors like us back in the fifties and sixties. When Dorothy Bender said her son was a doctor, why didn't I say that I'm one too?*

KAREN: *Because you are from Iowa. Nicey-nice and non-confrontive.*

MARGARET: *Shit. I hate that.*

KAREN: *You can't help it. But it's not good in the end.*

It is a cool spring Saturday afternoon. Karen is expecting an emergency patient — a couple from Shiloh. I'm on my way out to a fix-it project. We're in the kitchen of the big house.

"Do you know anything about the Shiloh Church?" I ask. Karen often knows these things from conversations with her various patients. I only know that their church school and dormitory is over south of Kalona, across the English River. Something about it being the largest free-standing, all-wooden building in Iowa. It's attracted many people from California, Colorado, Brazil and even New Jersey, where our landlords come from.

"Well I know that the original 'prophet' of the church was from just down the road in Washington, our county seat. In the late sixties or seventies, he had quite a ministry in California, among the lost beach kids, which he called the Church of the Living Word. After the sixties, many group leaders became paranoid and took their groups to refuge. Their church moved here when an Iowa farmer offered them acres just south of the English River. Many Californians about our age moved with him."

I remind her of local gossip. "People are worried about whether or not there are guns stored at the Shiloh compound, and there's talk of an underground tunnel to Iowa City."

Karen looks thoughtful. "Yeah, there is some mystery about them since you have to be invited to services — no dropping in. Lately, they've made an effort to integrate into the community with their Fourth of July musical and elaborate fireworks.

"In their worship, they tone together — a blending of voices meant to raise the vibration and spirit. Very California. They also practice what they call 'Waiting on the Lord,' which I believe is a form of channeling or opening the body to receive messages from noncorporeal entities. They say the communication comes from God, but in my opinion it can come from different hierarchical levels, even the ego. So discernment is required.

"I don't mention this to anyone else, because it would most likely elicit an extreme negative reaction from the locals who only seem to tolerate messages from their minister's interpretation of the Bible.

"They're Christian but celebrate holidays as Jesus would have celebrated them, so only Jewish holidays.

Shiloh means 'place of peace' in Hebrew. Meanwhile these Californians bring their talent and tech savvy to us here in the southeast corner of Iowa."

"OK, cool. That seems pretty sophisticated. Who is your patient?"

"Gary Bennett. Messed his back up skiing in Colorado."

"Well, good luck. I'll be out working on the driveway."

I head back out the kitchen door, through the garage to the Main Street side of our house. The driveway from our tiny garage meets the sidewalk and then slopes to the street. A rut has formed where the tires drop off as the car backs out. I am embedding bricks, like sturdy fringe, perpendicular to the sidewalk to reinforce it.

From my kneepad perspective, I see a family van pull up out front. A forty-something woman with short, henna-tinted hair gets out the driver's door and comes around to ease a tall blonde man from the passenger seat. He is bent over with pain, making his way toward the front door.

I continue troweling and reinforcing my bricks, thinking that it's fun to see patients our age since the demographic around us tends to be considerably older. As though to corroborate that thought, here comes a skinny, scowling woman striding down the sidewalk from up the hill. She is wearing a no-nonsense navy skirt and cardigan sweater over a prim white blouse. She stops, hovering above where I am working. I glance up and smile. A seventy-year-old face with an out-of-date pageboy peers down at me. "I'm Dorothy Bender. I live at the top of the hill," she announces. "My son is a doctor."

I straighten up to introduce myself. I take off a work glove to shake her hand as she turns away. "Well, that will never last," she says, flouncing on down the block, pronouncing doom on my project.

I finish seating the last scorned brick, then stand to unstrap my kneepads, gather my tools and survey my work. It looks pretty good to me to keep the drive from eroding away. Heading back toward the garage I stop to admire the little woodland garden under the kitchen window. A smoky-lipstick-colored trillium is fully open and the bleeding hearts are beginning to drip pink valentines. Further on, under the adjusting room window, the slim green leaves of the naked ladies are preening themselves for their opulent pink blush later in the summer. They seem optimistic. Me too.

Gary and Carol Bennett, the new patients, have left by the time I'm in the bath off the kitchen washing up. Karen sits at the kitchen table and I pour us mint hibiscus tea and slide the honey jar toward her side of the table.

"They were nice," she says, "he caught his ski, missed a turn, slammed his low back and hip. Psoas spasm plus ilium bruising. Got it to relax so I could get his pelvis aligned.

"They're from Colorado. Three kids in Mid-Prairie schools. It sounds like there are many parents our age at Shiloh — most from California. That could be a good reason for us to stay.

"I began my own inner journey in California. Actually it began the day I walked into a metaphysical bookstore and Jane Roberts' *Seth Speaks* fell off the shelf in front of me. That was a sign. Jane Roberts was the channel of Seth, the nonphysical entity talking about consciousness of an individual soul that sustains through lifetimes and is always available even if it is not obvious in the daily life. It's why I'm OK with the idea of channeling. I would be comfortable working with these folks. They seem to like us — might make it worthwhile for us to stay."

"Well, we won't be staying for the likes of Dorothy Bender," I say. "I met her as she was flouncing down the street. She made a point of insulting my brick-laying and telling me that her son is a 'doctor.'"

As I sip tea, I flip open this week's *Wellman Advance* lying on the table. "Ha! It says here that she is president of the Good Neighbor Committee for the Methodist church."

Karen rolls her eyes, "I'm sure she loves her own flock."

It seems that rational thought just wants to keep the emotional horizon level with a rational reason for even the strangest happenings.

Here We Go

At the kitchen table after Karen has received a package from Sue Ellen Johnson, her friend from the hygienic lab who owns a hobby farm outside of Iowa City. A couple weeks ago Karen and Margaret made a house call to attend to Waldo, Sue Ellen's Shar-Pei. That's a currently trendy Chinese breed, a medium-sized, toffee-colored, short-haired dog with a droopy muzzle, little triangular ears and tiny brown eyes rather lost in loose folds of skin around its head and shoulders that sort of resemble furry brain fissures. Waldo was paralyzed, and Sue Ellen had already spent his $500 stud fee for services not yet rendered.

KAREN: *Look here! It's a photo of Waldo! My first patient success and it's not even a person. God is he homely!*

MARGARET: *It's impressive that he's better. After seeing the X-ray of those two lumbar vertebrae rotated ninety degrees, it looked pretty perilous.*

KAREN: *Remember the Iowa State vet said it was raccoon fever.*

MARGARET: *Probably never read an X-ray for structural alignment. I'm sure it was a horse kick. But it was brilliant to teach her daughters to gently traction and lift that side. He looked pretty happy to be waited on though.*

KAREN: *Yeah. Sue Ellen said it took a bitch in heat to walk through the field to get him up and out the door on his own.*

And so it really begins, lifts right off over the course of the year, the idea of us sort of takes flight into the community — like putting Marge Hershberger's seventy-year-old farmwife body on the table with her butt elevated so Karen can gently lift her ischium, letting her relax into a favorable pain-free contour, easing the tension on her inflamed sciatic nerve. Well, OK, it's not right off in the sense that Marge does have to go back to her coffee group of Marilee Stout, the burly night nurse; Doris Hughes, the widowed plumber's wife; and Maxine Schrock, who also coffees at the drugstore every afternoon, to tell them with calculated bluntness, "She stuck her thumb up my butt while I was lying on my stomach, but it helped."

Then dynasties begin to arrive and the roots grow deeper. Our relationship with the Bowman family begins with a tense waiting room huddle over junior-high son Derek's future in sports. He's an intense, spare yet strong and agile kid. As a young teenager in a bright white T-shirt he doesn't say much, just points with a finely muscled arm to the area of pain in his head and neck so Karen can realign his atlas and that side-stepped wrongful curve using her spring-loaded adjusting tool. Now, four parents — his mother and her new husband, his father Kurt and his new wife Brenda — sit with Karen to weigh in on the subject of Derek and the sacrosanct topic of football.

I overhear a slice of conversation as I return from a day's work at the hospital. Apparently I've just missed pleas and entreaties inspired by their imaginings of

Derek's future athletic fame on the gridiron as a running back. The dads sit forward in earnest, their forearms flexed on their thighs. The moms lean toward their husbands in support of their projections and supplication.

Then it's Karen's turn. "Derek is athletic and strong," she says. "He's just not weighty enough to be playing against the massive kids out for football now." This appears to be something highly unusual — the undiluted, unvarnished truth from the plucky female chiropractor, who dares to speak anathema to the football dream fantasy world and four parents who do not agree on much of anything besides this. She continues, "Getting hit again and again by such big kids will not allow him to play to his potential and I imagine it will only get more dangerous as he gets older and the opponents are as much as a hundred pounds heavier."

She prevails in the end and he takes up wrestling, a rough and twisted sport but he is matched against someone in the same weight class. Hard feelings melt as Derek becomes a serious grappler. Meantime, Kurt, sort of a small bandy-legged roofer, and Brenda — taller, imposing, do-anything, some-time roofer, daycare owner and bus driver — become patients. They bring Brenda's children, her sister, mother, uncle and anyone she can drag through the door.

Then Edith Miller schedules to see Karen about a back strain from her work up at the toothbrush factory in Iowa City and simultaneously gets a long-time foot problem solved. She sends her sister Betty, soon-to-be owner of the Chat and Chew Bar, her son Jimmie, the plumber, and her husband Elvin, retired on disability. Turns out that the two sisters are the daughters of Mrs. Mennonite Woman who lived behind us down at Chester's. Everyone except Elvin, who has a degenerative nerve disease and a surgically fixed spine, has a good outcome and becomes either a monthly maintenance patient or we are their go-to if something goes wrong — like Jimmie making a strategic error showing off on his motorcycle and then dropping it and wrenching his back while trying to cavalierly pick it up.

All the while the elementary-school teachers — all women — have discovered they like low-impact adjusting and over time will even be adventurous enough to explore Emotional Balancing and acupuncture. They cheerfully turn up in their brightly colored sweaters and socks. Oddly enough, Karen sees no one from the high school except for the specialty teachers — the women's basketball coach, the choir and theatre directors — also all women. Do the conventional teachers' minds close in the higher grades or are they just sitting in adult-sized chairs and have no physical or emotional problems? I never do figure this out.

At the same time, the Shiloh reach continues to spread. Carol Bennett most likely sits with her long limbs folded comfortably at the reception desk of the Kalona Insurance Agency, a pencil nesting over her ear in her short, garnet-colored hair, thinking how much improved her husband is after his emergency clinic visit. So when her friend Wanda Pope, receptionist at an Iowa City dentist office, pops her smiling nonchalant prettiness through the door inquiring, "How did it go?" Carol beams. "I'm so relieved. He's doing much better."

And Wanda says, "Well, maybe I'll check it out, I keep getting headaches from sitting all day and then sitting in the damn bleachers for Tim's basketball games ... and I should tell my sister Barb."

So that's six adults and their seven growing athletic children. And soon the Wentworths, the Potters, the Fishers, the Olsons and, in no time, Patty, Connie, Lake, Leila, Jim, Peter and JJ. Not much at Shiloh is secret for long.

Sometime toward the end of a week Karen comes into the kitchen where I am sizzling onions and garlic with mustard and cumin seeds for a pot of spicy dal. "Mmm ... that smells good. And look here! My schedule is completely full next Monday!"

I look up to see her page filled with names from nine to seven before and after her two-hour lunch break. "That's terrific! You know for feng shui reasons people put fountains in the entryways of their businesses to attract clients and abundance. Maybe your photo of success patient Waldo at the front desk is bringing good fortune."

Why elucidate the specifics and magnitude of a destructive irrational belief unless it can be changed? Unless, I suppose, you're a poet or novelist.

It's My Elbow

MARGARET: *I stopped by the University of Iowa biology building to see my major professor today when I was up in the City. You remember John Menninger ... in his late fifties, tall guy with a wide impish grin, taught Cell Biology? You met him at ArtsFest last summer.*

KAREN: *Yeah, he was pretty nice. How did that go?*

MARGARET: *He's always cheerful. He seems to like me because I asked good questions in class. I tried to explain Emotional Balancing to him.*

KAREN: *How did that go?*

MARGARET: *Well, he listened politely, without really understanding much. He was encouraging in a not-that-I-can-help-you sort of way. He didn't say, "That sounds cool! How soon can I schedule?"*

Nancy Engelbright is a nondescript woman with drab brown hair and a small, kind of pinched, tense face — an easy-to-forget person whom I will never forget. She is apparently in for her third visit when Karen leaves her in the adjusting room and comes upstairs to consult. "Her knee is not holding its adjustment and I wonder if you could check some leg muscles to see if that's part of the problem?"

"Sure. I'll be right down. Look here, John Menninger just sent me this funny postcard and a reprint of H.L. Mencken essays. I've seen them before but never had a copy — H.L. Mencken weighs in on chiropractic in *The Baltimore Evening Sun*, 1924."

"Right. I can't wait. Meantime we need you."

"OK. I'm coming."

Downstairs, I'm introduced to thirty-eight-year-old impassive Nancy who is sitting up on the adjusting table wearing dark slacks and a faded blouse. Karen explains her problem. "Nancy has had this pain in her right knee for seventeen years. Ever since her knee-cap got slammed into the glove box in a car accident. I think she might have some weak muscles so she's not holding her adjustment."

"Nice to meet you, Nancy. What we're going to do is…" I explain that I'm going to place her leg in particular positions and ask her to hold while I apply counter pressure. "Let's begin with your quadriceps," I say as I tap her fleshy right thigh. "Lift your knee off the table and hold it in the air as I push on it." It collapses to the table. "This is a primary knee muscle so, let's give it some help. Place your fingertips here at the base of your ribcage. Good. Just like that. And again lift your knee off the table."

This time I push harder and the muscle easily holds her leg firm in marching band position. Her face cracks a bit as she grins and her eyes widen with surprise. We continue with muscles of hip, knee and ankle — the bad news of multiple weaknesses, followed by the good news of points that strengthen.

I draw the outline of a woman's body on a plain piece of paper and put little x's at points along the rib cage border, above the belly button, above the pubic bone and along the thighs.

"OK, for the next week why don't you massage these points three times a day? Then we'll recheck them and see how it's going." And off she goes with her paper.

Karen has finished with her last person and we meet for a supper — a simple antipasto of olives, greens and feta with a couple pieces of warmed up Swiss cheese quiche. We talk about our new experiment of applying the point/muscle relationships in a whole new way from how we were taught.

Then Karen wants to know, "So what was it Menninger sent you today?"

"It was a little package with a postcard and paperback book. The postcard has a 1950s woman in a low-cut, pink ruffled dress sitting at a white kitchen table, drinking a large glass of beer, eating a rich cheese sandwich with cookies, honey and mustard on the table, next to an ashtray with a pipe in it. The text box reads 'I said no to drugs but yes to booze, tobacco, junk food, fast driving and lots of makeup.' I don't know what to make of it, although it's cheerful. Anyway, the message on the back in his tiny-print script slanting somewhat downhill says, 'Margaret, I turned up this reprint of H.L. Mencken the other day and instantly thought that you and Karen might be amused. If nothing else it is an interesting historical attitude, as expressed by one of America's leading skeptics of the twentieth century, John Menninger.'

"He sent it because of *The Baltimore Sun* article from 1924, when Mencken takes on chiropractic. Here's the opening sentence and some condensed commentary under the title 'Chiropractic.' It begins: 'This preposterous quackery flourishes in the back reaches of the Republic and begins to conquer the less civilized folk of the big cities ... the chiropractic therapeutics rest upon the doctrine that the way to get rid of pinches (caused by misplaced vertebrae upon the spinal cord) is to climb upon a table and submit to a heroic pummeling by a retired piano mover.'

"Then he goes on about that quack Palmer taking up the idea after it was abandoned by that quack osteopath Still and 'teaching it to ambitious farmhands and out-at-elbow Baptist preachers in a few easy lessons.' It'll drive you nuts if I read you the whole thing, which has some truth of the times and occasionally placates but mostly skewers practitioners. So let's jump to the finale:

> Moreover, chiropractic itself is not certainly fatal: even an Iowan with diabetes may survive its embraces. Yet worse, I have a suspicion that it sometimes actually cures. For all I know ... it *may* be true that certain malaises are caused by the pressure of vagrum vertebrae upon the spinal nerves. And it *may* be true that a hearty ex-boilermaker, by vigorous yanking and kneading, may be able to relieve that pressure. What's needed is a scientific inquiry into the matter, under rigid test conditions by a committee of men learned in architecture and plumbing of the body and of a high and

incorruptible sagacity. Let a thousand patients
be selected, let a gang of selected chiropractors
examine their backbones and determine what
is the matter with them and then let these diagnoses be checked by the exact methods of scientific medicine. Then let those same chiropractors essay to cure the patient whose maladies
have been determined. My guess is that the
chiropractors' errors in diagnosis will run to at
least 95% and that their failure in treatment will
push 99%. But I am willing to be convinced.

"Then it ends with how he'll nominate the committee, provide the participants with music, cigars and
drink afterward and a banquet for the whole Medical
Trust when it's finished."

Never without a parry, Karen says, "They wouldn't
want to put us to the test or it would have happened
by now."

All week I am thinking of this article. I love the
expression "vagrum vertebra" for a wandering misaligned vertebra. The word quack was certainly in use
growing up in Davenport. But, when I had my first
chiropractic experience, with Dr. Gretchen Schreffler
in Iowa City, it was one of the most brilliantly subtle,
positive experiences in my life. It's flattering that my
professor has made this acknowledgment of us with
this communication. After all, it's out there. And there
remains so little true curiosity between professions that
I'm going to consider this a positive acknowledgment.

Karen continues her medical ripostes throughout the week: "Remember Chester telling us of old Doc Ainsworth who treated all kinds of people during the polio epidemic — went to their houses and adjusted them — and they survived with few negative effects? Only they never really paid him so he left to practice somewhere else. How scientific is it really when a person is prescribed multiple medicines simultaneously? Thousands of people die annually from fatal drug interactions. Didn't they stop doing postmortems after fatal illnesses because the diagnoses were often uncorroborated?"

Finally, the calendar turns. It's been a week since Nancy's visit and now we can see how the knee experiment went. She comes in with a brighter demeanor, a forceful stride, shiny hair and wearing a pink blouse. In her visit with Karen they apparently do not need me to do any follow-up. She pays and is dismissed. Karen continues her day.

A bit later I check with Karen, "Well, how did it go?"

"I asked how she was doing and she said, 'It's my elbow.' So I specifically asked about her knee, and she said, 'Oh yeah, it's fine.' She completely forgot she had that knee problem for all that time. So, I check a couple muscles and now her knee is holding in place. I adjust her elbow and dismiss her. I guess that's our answer."

I am riveted with the implications of this splendid outcome. "Wow! Seventeen years of pain gone and forgotten in a week! How great is that? I guess pain that is gone is really that forgettable.

A negative belief can cause physical symptoms like a rash, sleeplessness or low back pain.

Expanding Horizons

MARGARET: *Did you ever read those Ayn Rand books, The Fountainhead and Atlas Shrugged?*

KAREN: *No, well, I guess I did, but they didn't impress me. I mostly read science fiction — Ursula Le Guin and Robert Heinlein.*

MARGARET: *Well I did. I was an unformed person then, susceptible to strong attractive individualists — their snobbery, frigid judgments and rational self-interest. Luckily, I was subsequently soothed by earthy, heroic hobbits in The Lord of the Rings.*

KAREN: *Didn't read those. I moved on to mysteries.*

MARGARET: *The feeling I had with the Ayn Rand characters was like trying to understand a definition from a 1950s dictionary which was so rational and inhospitable it could wring the life out of any word. Her disparagement of altruism really lassoed me and subdued some brightness within me. Made me cynical and have to double think my actions in a way I didn't really appreciate ... And I became terribly worried about being found naïve.*

I swing out of the driver's seat of my Dodge Caravan. My blue-and-white **WELLWMN** license plate overbites the parking curb at National College of Chiropractic here in Lombard, Illinois, suburb of Chicago, four and a half hours from home. The engine ticks warmly in the early Saturday afternoon as I do some knee bends at the open car door, then stretch and grasp my bag for an afternoon of sitting in class. The parking lot has a Cadillac, an Audi, a Mercedes, two shiny pick-ups and several more nondescript cars like mine.

I hustle past a decorative water feature along a manicured lawn and up cement steps into a gray gran-ite building because now I'm late — maybe only fifteen minutes behind. Let's see, Lecture Room 6. Yes, just here on the left and … Hey, I'm not late. The room is large with a wall of windows and individual blonde desks that look roomy enough to be comfortable even if they can only be accessed from the left. I slow to a nonchalant pace barely noticed by twenty or so most-ly male, all-white classmates waiting attentively for class to begin. I notice a dark-haired, olive-complected woman sitting behind two long tables at the rear of the room doing the administrative duties.

I choose a seat on the middle aisle halfway back, put my leather cruising bag in the seat and water bottle on the desk, then turn to sign in. The woman smiles and says her name, which is something like Jalashree, and asks for mine.

"It's so nice to meet you," she says in an exotic, matronly manner. She finds my name on the list of pre-paid students and hands me two packets of notes — Introduction to Acupuncture and The Lung and Large Intestine Meridians. She has laid out a mini bookstore of eight or ten impressive textbooks, several point charts and boxes of acupuncture needles. It instantly becomes clear there is a lifetime of study here. I prepare to open the closest book, but now there is a whir of activity at the front of the room. I scuttle my notes to my seat as Dr. Jon Sunderlage, middle-aged, linebacker-shaped guy with a receding hairline and dark combed-back, no-style hair, ordinary brown suit trousers and a white long-sleeved shirt, sleeves rolled twice on sturdy ex-farmboy forearms, steps to the side of the podium. From behind metal aviator-type glasses he smiles a no-apology greeting to the class.

We discover that he runs a clinic in a suburb near here and keeps Saturday morning hours, which is why I will not rush to get here for the beginning of class since I see that he will also be late. He is a kinesiology chiropractor using acupuncture training he received in China. He has a bounty of stories from his own clinic patients and those Chinese clinics, including videos from that inscrutable world. I'm ready to step along with him on a fearless journey.

He begins the introduction to this foreign language — this ancient art involving yin/yang, heat/cold, full/empty; pathways of electrical connection, like maps with great metropolises, small towns, even railroad crossings; the continuum of the five elements — Wood, Fire, Earth, Metal and Water, their daily and seasonal cycles and their nurturing and combating relationships. In this world, an illness becomes an imbalance. The state of the body affects the mind; the state of the mind affects the body. I have seen this in Balancing.

Later that first afternoon, we buy boxes of needles from Jalashree who is introduced as his invaluable assistant, which to me means his work wife. He's a lucky guy. The class moves to a lab room with bench tables. We open our needle packages, locate a simple site, then stab, well, insert them in ourselves.

I'm sharing a table with Josh. He's a bit taller than me, athletic, with soft brown eyes and a neat, trim beard and wearing a gold wedding band. I'm only paying attention to the web between my thumb and first finger and the zing I feel, when he utters a strange sound and I realize that he's become quite woozy and unsteady from the needling lesson. He bends forward with his head down. I put a hand on his shoulder and offer him some water. After a brief restorative moment, he accepts a drink, runs his hand through his hair and across his beard and says, "I'm going to have to practice this in my hotel tonight." That will be some help but tomorrow we will be putting needles in each other.

And so the yearlong class begins. Each weekend after class I am more energized than when we began because we treat each other in the lab.

Acupuncture is illegal for chiropractors in the state of Iowa, from some old 1970s law allowing chiropractors to do venipuncture for lab tests, yet disallowing acupuncture. By the time class is complete and I have my initial certification, the chiropractic board has made acupuncture legal for us.

I find other seminars in Minneapolis and St. Louis, and then with the acclaimed Richard Yennie, chiropractor acupuncturist in Kansas City. He's a dark-eyed, wavy-haired Scotsman who has taken on a Chinese-like caricature with narrowed flashing eyes and a toothy smile. I think he was a Japanese translator during WWII who returned to the U.S. ready to take up law, but then had a life-changing experience that brought him to chiropractic. He learned Chinese and studied acupuncture in China. Now he has a large classroom built on to his clinic in downtown Kansas City. He, too, has a work wife, plus a sizable staff and, at seventy-something, also has a young, blonde, showpiece wife.

One of his interns begins class with forty-five minutes of Qi Gong. He occasionally brings in athletes from the KC Chiefs to tell their stories and he often allows students to share new innovative techniques. His throwaway lines of philosophy are as interesting as the subject, like "If you know what you're doing every minute, you're not learning," or "Only fools and dead men don't change their minds."

Even without being actual mentors, these teachers are open, flexible and daring, and this imparts confidence. I read my textbooks during my free time, lucky that the principles work even in the hands of a novice. So with a ready-made clientele and Karen's interest in the expansion it gives to our practice, I let go of my hospital job and find it instantly forgettable.

There is a little bump in the road as my acquaintance Ellen Williamson, LAc (Licensed Acupuncturist), from the City challenges me as the upstart who didn't spend three years in acupuncture school. I explain the nature of my studies and assuage her professional ego;

I am a humble practitioner within the scope of my chiropractic license and expertise. We part amiably.

And now it's the beginning of a practice — supporting Karen's patients: the roofer with the herniated disc whose mother had to help him through the garage backdoor entrance since he couldn't manage the front steps and the woman who avoids neck surgery by getting adjusted, learning her muscle points and having intermittent acupuncture on her neck and upper back.

Then comes seventy-three-year-old retired teacher Alice, leaning on her husband's arm, in from the depth of a snowy winter day. She wants to avoid surgery for the yam-sized tumor on her sacrum. When I say this is not in the scope of my practice she says, "I told them I didn't want surgery." So I agree to treat her.

"What is going to happen to it?" she asks.

I think that there is no one to ask this question of since anyone else would have it removed. "Well," I say, "It will either go in or go out."

And it turns out that with two treatments it essentially does both. Although I do not see this, her husband reports that it develops a fissure down the center, cracks open, and drains its serous innards. Then the sides begin to curl and shrivel like dried leaves. After the second visit she calls to ask if acupressure will work as well. "Sure, it could," I say.

She disappears into the January cold and I only hear a year or so later that she's gone to live with her daughter and let herself fade from life. I like what I learned from her. I like that she had the choice, a discernment of sorts, to muster and regain her strength or to fall back on her husband's supportive arm and slip away.

Then the practice grows for a variety of issues: sinus problems, lung recovery, digestion, skin inflammations, body aches and pains. Often these conditions can be aided or ameliorated. There is a young woman named Heather getting regular kidney dialysis who comes as a last-minute punt since she's waiting for a kidney transplant. She's kind of like someone with end-stage cancer or dementia whose family abruptly decides to try something "alternative." Generally, it's poor timing, although sometimes there is a palliative response. It's not usually the miraculous turnaround they are looking for. But Heather is only in her thirties, the victim of fanatic, destructive dieting regimes and terrible, erratic food choices. With regular treatments and finding a way to eat regular healthy meals, in a couple months she has resumed normal kidney function.

We enrich our country practice with a treatment that expands from structural, physical and emotional into electrical harmony. It's also good timing that there is lots of good press about acupuncture these days, much better than we've ever experienced for chiropractic.

I notice that besides learning how people's beliefs are constructed, each Balance has a positive energetic effect on me.

Geraldine and Two Orvilles

Morning cracks open across our Midwestern countryside. Newborn sunbeams shine afresh on the altered landscape and burdened soils.

KAREN: *You look better today ... better than that taciturn-bald-eagle I-am-smiling face you had yesterday.*

MARGARET: *I am better. I gave myself a Balance yesterday. I'd been feeling uneasy on multiple levels — kind of depressed about getting to know the many struggles in this community and oddly self-conscious about my body.*

KAREN: *So did you Balance for them separately?*

MARGARET: *I took a shot at combining them as one goal — to fill my Body and Life with Love. And guess what? When I was holding points for the heart meridian, I felt mySelf become the earth — a Body of mountains, lakes and thoroughfares full of trees and flowers and vibrant teeming life ... So today I'm refreshed and OK to continue in this dimension and place.*

Geraldine sits with slumping posture on my upstairs table — no doubt just what Karen has suggested she try to not do. She's wearing a forest-green sweater and matching pants from well back in her closet. She's here for what might translate as sagging shoulders and a depressed outlook, although she's married to an heir to the Schroeder Ag fortune with an expanse of acres south of town. We have not met her husband though we know her sister-in-law, Vickie, who is one of our cheerful schoolteachers and a faithful patient.

Geraldine seems rather confused about why she doesn't have friends. "I guess when I'm not occupied with chores and farrowing, I'll just have to invite the neighbor women over for coffee," she says, with a brief stirring from her daze.

"I think you would benefit from some supportive conversation," I say. But I'm unable to fully embrace her version of that idea when I begin to work out that perhaps this is old thinking, like from forty-some years ago when she was a young girl. That's back when there were still some neighbors besides Vickie and her husband on down the windy highway.

I begin to realize she is a lonely queen of the mountain with a huge farm and giant pork operation. Is it possible that she doesn't quite realize that her neighbors are either gone — their land auctioned to the other giant farms around them when interest rates skyrocketed — or at work in their one or two jobs and farming at night just trying to preserve the few acres they have held onto? Can it be true that the boom of land prices, subsequent high-dollar borrowing and then the crush of bankruptcies of the 1980s farm crisis have happened all around her without her realizing the consequences? I guess it could be a survivor's delusion. Plus, she's in big and bigger Ag now with feed deliveries, vet bills, scales, piggy pharmaceuticals and massive raw sewage disposal.

She doesn't discuss any mechanics of farm function with me and doesn't seem to have a determining voice in them. For this farm wife, it's now more of a job for tall rubber boots and a syringe than for gardening gloves and the smells of loamy soil in a garden of fresh peas, cabbages, potatoes and radishes.

"So, let's talk about options to brighten your outlook," I say. "A good multivitamin, maybe extra B ... Do you use real yogurt? Have 'green stuff' for supper? How can you get some fun physical activity?"

She has a passing glimmer of interest and a transient pretty smile with the idea of involvement in groups or getting regular exercise. "I could go to Curves," she says, looking down at her lap without admiration, "or join a stitchery club. I have done some quilting and cross stitch." Whereupon I think of rare visits to my sister's place and her walls filled with her stitchery creations — fabulous, intricate, pictorial, shiny-beaded, complicated — and I cannot really feel the longing within Geraldine.

Each activity begins to sound like an involved drive to town that she doesn't seem likely to spiff up for, like some of the other farm women do. I feel a torpid weight descend on the ideas before they've fully formed. She's clearly not going to go walking along the treeless, boring sameness of their highway. Her mood flattens again. Our talk has not buoyed her spirits or elevated her emotionally. She leaves without rescheduling. I feel the pull of pharmaceuticals will win her over in the end and douse this moment of curiosity for improvement. Somehow, if all this economic change has happened around her without her realizing it, she may not be able to find initiative now.

I feel an opposite sense of trust in the natural world when the Orvilles meet in our clinic waiting room later that afternoon. Eighty-year-old Orville Rediger and I are coming down the staircase from the upstairs treatment room. He's just had acupuncture to improve his touchy digestion and relieve his gnarled, overused fingers. He smiles down into the front room. "Well look who's here." His face crinkles in recognition of two other old-geezer farmers down below.

Orville Penningroth and Harold Gingerich pepper him with questions as he joins them. "How's Roxanne?" "Did you get that little Harvester tractor sold?" "You speakin' to Milton yet?"

The other Orville is short, with combed-back white hair, wearing striped overalls and a bright white T-shirt. He and his brother have a place at the edge of town where they raise shorthorn beef cattle and black-with-white Poland China hogs.

I once went to an early spring swine auction in their faded-white sloping barn with bleacher seating that cleverly folded down from the rafters. Donnie Bohr, their surrogate grandson and farmhand, showed me to a seat. "Are you a journalist?" He asked with a rather hopeful smile as I delicately negotiated the planks. I thought that would be some fun, but said no.

I asked him to interpret the program for me. His barnyard-tan forefinger pointed to the pertinent info on each young hog. "Here are the specs on each one," he said. "They're being auctioned for breeding stock." He liked having his prizes appreciated and explained the difference between gilts, barrows, sows and boars. I learned that the number listed next to each of the boars and gilts was the number of teats, reflecting their reproductive capacity. A minor epiphany! A sunny-faced boy helped me grasp the value of tits on a boar.

The very last little gilt did not sell because she had a limping back leg. I wondered if she might have performed better had she been adjusted beforehand.

My patient Orville has sun-dried, pecan-colored neck and arms. He wears a faded striped feed cap and a short-sleeved plaid cotton shirt, revealing his lean muscles and old-man white forearm hairs. We've bonded as members of the CCI — Citizens for Community Improvement. It's a group making people aware of the truths of factory hog farming — thousands of carefully hybridized many-teated sows full of antibiotics, hormones and industrially designed feed, penned inside so they can't even turn round, standing over the raw sewage collection pit for subsequent spreading on surrounding acres. CCI is a vigorous little organization, aware that we are sacrificing our communities and our land and water quality so more and more Chinese can eat pork daily. But it's fairly helpless in the wake of a mighty corporate push for profits and the slipstream of integrated production.

Orville is chagrined that his older brother Milton has recently become the talk of the town for selling his part of the family acres to Clyde Olmstead. Clyde has bankrupted himself in a previous business, leaving many townspeople with uncollectible debt. He is now in the steel-building business and is going to put a huge factory hog farm on his newly acquired property just north of town. And, no, Orville's not talking to him quite yet.

I don't know the third man with the Orvilles. Harold, with curly gray hair and a constant look of surprise on his old, lined face. Maybe I've heard that his wife is not quite all right. The three of them shake hands and politely joke with each other. Solidarity of a sort, I guess, since they are the last of the nonAmish who disdain this new factory farming. Between them are over two hundred years, a sea of acres, bushels of confidence and an unmentioned sense of their legacy being plowed under by corporate bulldozers.

Karen strolls out. "Orville. I'm ready for you," she says.

He smooths his white hair and smiles. Turning to his friends he says, "Good to see you, Orville. Guess I'll see you later, Harold. Don't forget that concentrated cherry juice for your gouty feet." The other two walk out together sharing a conversation that's been going on a long, long time.

What I know about farming is pretty insufficient, subject to ridicule, actually, by those who've willingly accepted the corporate line, who call me out as a naïve intruder from the outside. But, I know that the Orvilles' priorities are on perfecting their breeds and enhancing their soils, not falling into the chemicalized farming trap. Just as we rely on quality nutrition, optimal structural support and emotional strengthening for our results instead of instant pharmacology, I see them as a trustworthy heritage in overalls and feed caps. The synchronicity of these old patriarchs meeting in our waiting room on this day is a wistful glimpse into a passing world.

It must be denial when a person's body agrees that something is true and, at the same time, agrees that the person must act as though it is not true.

Bill and Mary

Margaret comes down to the kitchen for morning coffee. Karen, lying facedown on her adjusting table, calls out.

KAREN: *Honey!? Can you help me?*

MARGARET: *What's the matter, babe?*

KAREN: *I can't turn my head and my first patient comes in an hour.*

MARGARET: *Oh that's terrible. OK, let's see what we can do. Hold out your arm and let me muscle-test these vertebrae. Hmm, looks like you've got a couple of anterior thoracics and some muscle spasm. Stand up here with your back to this wall. Let me put a hand between your spine and the wall just under those vertebrae. Now bring your elbows together so I can use them to push. Round your shoulders, tuck your chin and take a breath. Now gently relax, let your breath go. I'll just give a little ... There that's good. Now massage here at the front of your upper arms ... unh hunh, then under both collarbones and along your sternum.*

KAREN: *Ouch! But better.*

Sixty-year-old Bill Wagamon is the Wellman Phone Company's general manager, also Karen's first patient of the day. And yet, the first person through the door is Mary Wagamon. Her short, wide, vigorous body has a kindly square face in a determined grimace as husband Bill leans on her shoulder. When upright he's nearly six feet tall and he's used to being the sparkly extrovert. When feeling good, he has laughing eyes behind his aviator-type glasses. He has a trim nose that has only been broken once despite numerous boxing matches and other pugilistic encounters. He's wearing his WWII 82nd airborne paratrooper ball cap, a white T-shirt and Chicago Cubs navy-blue sweatpants. At the moment he's gray and irritable with pain.

"You probably can't help me, but I thought I'd try this," he says to Karen. "Billy, my lineman, said I should come for my migraine headaches."

Karen will hear that opening line, "You probably can't help me..." many, many times. Without retort, she just guides them to a seat.

"Well, as soon as you fill out this paperwork we'll begin," she says.

Bill and his wife huddle together on the couch, knees touching, to confide and consult as Mary, efficient, retired home ec teacher, fills out Bill's patient history form on the clipboard. When done he tries to smile, a wide curtain of lips drawing back from white teeth, but halts midway as his forehead furrows with pain. They go into the adjusting room together, traveling as a pair like human guinea hens in a slow-motion scurry. I hang out for just a bit because when Karen has a problem like she did this morning, her first patient of the week often shows up with the same problem we have just addressed.

It turns out they don't need me today. Maybe the spell is breaking. When they reappear, Karen says, "It was his terribly rotated atlas, we didn't need to throw him against the wall after all."

They both look a little startled at her imagery, but Bill is glowing and immediately warms to the idea of a little sparring. "I'm ready. I did a little boxing in the service," he says, with that big looming smile. "I've had a chance to use it a bit since then." His eyebrows rise in joyful memory even as he feigns a cloak of sheepishness and looks to Mary. She sets her mouth in a familiar wrinkle of pretend frustration and gives an affectionate eye roll. Mostly she looks relieved.

"You know I really do feel better," he says, running his hand through his short gray hair before putting his cap back on. He may be surprised that we are not surprised.

He pauses a moment to consider. "You know, my aunt, Mrs. Murphy, used to own the house two doors up from you girls. I rode my horse in from the country to go to school back in the thirties. When it snowed too much I would stay there for the night and be close to the school in the morning."

The very same little one-room Smith Creek School, with its fresh white façade, warm wooden interior and Franklin wood stove is still preserved by the historical society, a block over and up a block up from our house. I have peered into its high windows, imagining three feet of snow outside and white chalk puffs and wood smoke smells on the inside.

Bill seems to be feeling himself again, like he could settle in for quite a conversation. "Now, Bill, don't get carried away," says Mary. "We need to let these doctors get back to work."

Karen hands him an appointment card. "I'd like to check you again next week. We want this to become your body's new habit. Does this time work for you?"

"Sure does, Doc. We'll see you then."

We cannot yet imagine how these two loving characters will become our friends, allies and confidants in ways our parents never could or would. Bill comes for adjusting when he sprains his ankle as a giant hay bale flattens him to the ground and rolls over his entire body. They commiserate with Karen about Gordon the banker and local business dealings. They come for vitamins and consolation when the neighboring farms' chemical spray causes him an allergic response.

One afternoon Bill calls from a grocery store in Washington. "Dr. Margaret, Mary is having a nervous attack. She feels faint and breathless."

Not good, I think. Knowing how she responds emotionally to things, I ask, "Is she unusually worried about something, Bill?"

"Yep. She has her annual physical in two days up at University Hospital."

She seems to be having her annual response. "OK, come right over, I'll have time in about forty minutes."

They come, this time with Mary comforted and supported by Bill. There's tension in her eyes, which normally glow blue and bright. She hyperventilates a bit. Her blood pressure is already starting to spike.

Even so, she prefers to sit on the table instead of

lying down. I arrange a treatment pattern of needles for her. She settles down and her color evens out. "Oh, Dr. Margaret," she says, "there's a new doctor almost every time I go, just when I've gotten comfortable with the last one. They interrogate me like I'm lying when I tell them I don't take any medications. Then I get so nervous about the tests they're going to run that my blood pressure goes sky-high. It's still two days away and I'm already a nervous wreck."

"It'll be OK, Mary. You're going to be fine to go for your appointment."

Then, a few weeks later, Bill gets himself into a situation because he'll do anything for his staff members — in this case, defending the husband of a woman who works for him. Except this time, it turns out the husband really is guilty of sexual abuse of a young girl at their church. Luckily, before he punches anyone, another friend intervenes to convince him. Then he's disgusted with the husband. Much later still, Bill gets an Emotional Balance when he retires from the phone company and temporarily loses his identity.

Their married daughter lives in a Chicago suburb so it's an easy trip for their tall teenage grandson to visit each summer. They remain unaffected and sincere, holding hands as they pray before a meal, sharing stories about Allie, the dog, playing with the barn cats, about Bill's favorite cow, about Mary's brother who inherited everything and doesn't chip in to help their other disabled brother, about politics and the perils of Big Ag. Turns out Bill listens to the paranormal program Coast to Coast AM on late-night WHO radio.

Our parents — Karen's uncharitable military family and my daily overdrinking dad and his replacement wife — have no interest in us. We appreciate Bill and Mary's fond, old-fashioned and wholly unfamiliar friendship.

Turns out it's not uncommon for a person to have come to believe that she, or even he, is responsible for every-thing, everybody all the time — even though this is com-pletely impossible and keeps the person from acting from her Truth.

Bill and the Feminist

Margaret is driving the white 940 Volvo station wagon — the one that looks like a white enamel/chrome piece of Scandinavian furniture — up to the City. Karen is getting dropped off to get her glasses adjusted and then have a brief, but fulfilling, shop at Discount Records, Vortex Crystal and Gem and Prairie Lights Bookstore.

KAREN: *I'll probably be a couple hours.*

MARGARET: *No problem. I'll stop at the New Pioneer Co-op first, then meet you at the Java House ... I'm writing morning pages you know.*

KAREN: *Whatever keeps the neurosis at bay.*

Margaret winces a grin, then leans across to give Karen a public kiss on her sweet, truth-telling little mouth.

MARGARET: *And shopping should give you a little worldly participation, plus you can pick up Machaelle Small Wright's* Behaving as if ...

KAREN: *Yes ...* the God in all Life Mattered.

In the coffee shop entryway with old-timey mosaic floor tiles, the smooth brass handle opens the worn wooden door to clinks and tinklings of silver and dishware and the welcoming aromas of coffee, cinnamon and flaky pastries. Beneath the high tin ceiling, in a long gray-walled room surrounded by black-and-white portrait prints, students tend to their notebooks or huddle in groups of twos and threes. Near the dark wooden ordering counter, newspapers from the larger world array on wands next to magazines with protective plastic covers. I feel the relief of impersonal contact and the welcome of uninterested strangers.

After a few minutes perusing the headlines of the President Bill and Monica scandal (wondering what didn't make the first page because of it), of awards for *Shakespeare in Love* and accolades for hockey great Wayne Gretzky, I hear "double Cuban macchiato" and step up to pick up my steaming little cup, saucer and tiny spoon. I set my place with the coffee and a croissant oozing butter and honey on a tall wooden table under a black-framed print. It's a delicate-lined portrait of a curly haired, expressionless white man staring off to my right, the lines more interesting than the visage portrayed. Well as long as he's not staring at me.

A few bites and sips, then I get out the current well-used composition notebook for what Julia Cameron calls the Morning Pages. Her prescription? Write three pages daily to clear the mind, put words to emotions. I open to the next blank page, not really caring about what's on the previous ones, and begin today's verbal riff, or maybe riffraff, combing through tangled strands of memory and impressions for clarity:

> *Been thinking about the Wagamons. It's weird how*
> *Bill laughs and talks the way he does, so appreciative,*
> *so supportive and happy to know us as independent*
> *rule-breakers, bragging about being on the vanguard of*
> *acupuncture among his friends, that wide-mouth grin,*

and calling me Dr. Squirt in the office. Now that he's been getting acupuncture, he forgets that it was Karen's adjusting that got rid of his headaches and I have to remind him, but he doesn't seem to care. His heart is in the right place; he's a great supporter of women's issues and is always in defense of Mary or his daughter. He loves his cows, is scared about the Farm Bureau and chemical farming. Their neighbors have deliberately doused their land with chemical spray when the plane lingers too long with the sprayer on before ascending. It would happen in some measure anyway with herbicide/pesticide/fungicide drift just because they own fewer than a hundred acres surrounded by mega farms. Still, his words do perturb me with how self-conscious I am about political correctness, since being outside the entrenched feminist community up here in the City means I will make impolitic mistakes and surely calling me Dr. Squirt and laughing is considered politically incorrect and inappropriate, but it's funny and sincere; even if it's juvenile flattery it counts for a lot from a guy his age, just an internal embarrassing quandary for me when I think back to the prescriptive ways of Iowa City's early attitudes of feminism. Even then, there was a sort of judgment and measuring up, as in who's most oppressed, Puggy Pressley? (My old friend Puggy — didn't we have fervent conversations about the evolving feminist milieu?) My current view of judgment is that it's a recipe for warped and competitive behavior. Common for churches and authoritarian groups because in judging others there is collective belonging. But there is

*simultaneously an unspoken fear of being judged your-
self, so you are steered down a narrow hardpan road
of conformity and twat-tightening and ball-bursting
because it's often about sexual things, which are universal. But instead of praising humanness with blessings of
love, it is remonstrated, mocked and judged, humiliated,
belittled or seized upon as an outrage by someone who
is no tender, kind, blessed goddess, but rather someone
who lives in the authority, often hypocritical authority
of their domain to make your life miserable. So, control
somebody's sexuality and you also have their creativity
and initiative — that is until it "pops out" of its own
irrepressible volition, then it betrays and reveals them in
ways warped from lovely human longings and self-ac-
tualized behavior. Judgment neutralizes the thoughtful
and intelligent into paroxysms of self-consciousness
and becomes one more level of misery for women who
have each experienced some sort of subjugated and
fucked-overness already by a patriarchal system that
despises our presence when there is a man to compare
to or defer to and there is not food to be served or some
cleaning up to do. Because of the judgment, some of us
learned to hide, learned to defer to men, respond with
nervous laughter instead of a true and adequate response. We learned that the men were going to get the
mentoring and the special deals or the special treatment,
while we were going to get superficial flattery and lip
service, no support in our second-tier jobs, and when we
woke up to what had happened, and what continues to
happen, and did our best to emerge from this comatose*

*place of lesser thinness, whatever that is, we became
mad. Sometimes we became neurotic, guilty or self
conscious first, but eventually we became mad which
we did not know how to do very well, or had been told
it wasn't ladylike, so you could be mad and unladylike,
which made you more like a dyke, but not really, just to
those who were upset at your unladylikeness, which was
pressuring them to give you a space at the table where
there was truly plenty of room, but few of us knew that
because we had learned that economics was all about
lack and not about abundance for all, and it required our
own competitiveness and what did that matter when
we were just seeking our place of aspiration within our
right to pursue happiness, intent on our own liberties
and not infringing upon yours except when your team
wanted more than it's share and our lives and bodies
were aggressed upon instead of having the opportunity
to share the abundance. Meantime the abundance was
being consolidated in the hands of . . .*

"Hey, Margaret, is that you? What are you doing
up here?"

My pencil flies from the concatenation of colliding
thoughts. The overflowing stream of words softly dis-
sipates among the coffee vapors.

"Why Patti McCord! Nice to see you! Karen and
I are up to the City for the afternoon. Grab a coffee.
Come join me."

"OK, sure." She flops her green army jacket, bou-
clé cap and worn book bag over the chair and moves

to the line. Her nape-length blonde hair sticks up in places from the static electricity. I shut the cover to my composition book, but the written-on pages are no longer smooth. They curl and undulate, burdened with the firm, penciled words disgorged in flurries into their rugged fibers.

Patti has been a patient of Karen's. Her constant reading and toiling for a PhD has her neck unconsciously coiled over feminist tomes, stretching her splenium capiti in a vice-like grip from the nape of her neck to the base of her skull, leading to constant headaches, all in the name of Women's Studies. I only know her in passing, as I see her small frame stride through the waiting room in Doc Martin purple leather shoes and short skirt over patterned tights. She returns to the table with a large latte cup and a perfunctory grin.

"Saturday is my day to study à la coffee house."

"What are you working on?"

"Well, my final project is …" And she emits a practiced stream of unemotional, scholarly words of an arid polemic, as I wish for the heart crush of an Adrienne Rich poem.

"But I meant to tell you of an encounter I had in Wellman when I was down your way for RVAP. The Rape Victim Advocacy Program sends women to Washington County for fundraising and to make sure that people know that we serve them too."

"Oh it does?" I say. "That's good to know." Even if she didn't actually share that information with us as a professional office. "How was your visit to the nether county?" I imagine her handsome woman/girl self among the small town denizens with her intense golden-brown eyes focused on her purpose, and their focus on her.

"Well, it went fairly well. But it was a real trip dealing with that Bill Wagamon of the Wellman Telephone Company."

I think *Oh Bill, what now? Are you going to compound my fears of you and political correctness?*

"Yes. I know him well," I say. "What happened?"

"Well he seemed very receptive at first. He was sensitive and respectful even. But then he called me a little heifer."

And here it is: the collision of worlds not just within me but manifesting in real time. "Oh, I see. Well he does love his cows."

I've decided, now, that I believe everything. It seems requisite to helping a person change their inner process — to truly understand.

Hazel and Oldness

MARGARET: *I've been thinking about my mom. One of these years I'm going to grow older than she was when she self-destructed. That's not something that's supposed to happen.*

KAREN: *She was fifty-six? How did she lose her grip?*

MARGARET: *Well, there was my dad who never knew how to care for her, and her church which just wanted her to serve it … and never learning to drive. Then the headaches and inner-ear dizziness. Can you imagine what my emotionally fragile menopause would have been like if I drank port with my morning coffee, smoked cigarettes, took no supplements, hardly ate, then finished the day with a few bourbon cocktails and some chocolates? Plus, remember all those drugs that were in her medicine chest when she died? You could have dumped them down the toilet and gotten half the city of Davenport high.*

KAREN: *In other words, if she'd been our patient she would not have had most of those problems. Well, you are going to do much better.*

Hazel is a grand old farm lady from Washington, twenty miles across the forever fields from Wellman. She's one of the few old women I come to know pretty well.

She is a richly uncommon character, at the same time typical of end-of-the-century rural Iowa where the dwindling population is aging. Most of the children and grandchildren are long gone, from lack of opportunity and adventure. I have no experience with older people and, in the time we've been here, I only learn that they are each a journey unto themselves.

I remember one ancient woman from my inhalation therapist days back in the late sixties. She was a small, seemingly fragile thing, lying eyes closed and unmoving, engulfed in white hospital sheets. I was supposed to give her a breathing treatment, although I'm not sure why. She had no respiratory diagnosis and was not post-surgery. Reluctant, but persisting, I touched her tiny arm and told her, "My name is Margaret and I'm here to give you a breathing treatment. I'm going to place this mask over your nose and mouth so you can inhale the treatment mixture."

No response. That is until I placed it over her nose and mouth and the machine whirred, spitting out an aerosol of saline. Then she came alive with a whole-body wince. She was no longer passively lying there. She'd become a startled creature in vigorous protective recoil. I kind of hope I'll do the same if I'm ever in such a position. Immediately I withdrew the mask and wrote in her chart "patient refuses treatment," a little embarrassed that I interrupted her peaceful agedness.

I have no theories about the elderly except their lives are like Yogi Berra's baseball aphorism, *not over 'til they're over*. I watch our immediate neighbor to the south who has a small two-chicken coop out back during the summer that she brings into her basement in the winter. A sturdy, fleshy woman in her late eighties, she sits on her front porch most summer evenings and watches the bits of comings and goings. Then, one day she isn't there and I hear from her daughter-in-law, who is Karen's patient, that she has fallen, broken her hip and is recovering in the home. The know-it-all part of me thinks *Well, this is the end for her.* But next summer she's back on her porch, and the next, and, well, at least six more summers, until she passes at ninety-six.

Hazel usually pulls up to the clinic in a spotless, long, white Dodge sedan, but not today. "I'm in the red mood this week," she says, as she smiles across the front door threshold in a lavender tracksuit, red leather handbag over one long, lean folded arm. I glance out to the curb and there's another showy four-door sedan, this one a lipstick-red Buick.

"How many cars do you have anyway?"

"Just the two," she says, pursing up her lower lip into a satisfying grin, arched dark brows lifting over her silver eyeglasses. "I've only got a two-car garage."

She has been going to chiropractors most of her long life. After seeing Karen for a neck issue that is easily resolved when she puts a small cushion in the driver's seat of each of those spotless sedans, she then becomes my patient for acupuncture tune-ups, asking, "Do you think you can help my sinuses and post-nasal drip?" Her melodic voice has a slight vibrato, her pale gray eyes ever curious.

We climb the carpeted stairs to the upstairs adjusting room. She is pretty agile at eighty-nine, with shoulders only slightly rounded so she is no longer the five-foot-eleven-inch height she once was. Sitting tall in the armchair she takes off her black Skechers and white socks.

"Anything new to concentrate on today?"

"The usual, I think. It seems to be helping my sinuses and this poor old thumb joint." She holds up her left hand, large with well-formed, strong fingers. The first knuckle of her thumb is misshapen with arthritic buildup. I insert the needles, then say, "I'll get your next supply of allergy supplement," and leave her alone for a while to absorb the energy of the needle arrangement.

She's comfortable talking so we always make a little time for that. Over the years, I learn that she's outlived her husband, a farmer and pilot who took her flying. She especially loved the white sands around Albuquerque. Her only son died in some sort of motor vehicle crash, so now there's one cousin left in her family. They get together with another friend or two to eat out in Washington once a week. "We call ourselves the Sunshine Girls," she says. "No going on about illnesses and catastrophes ... just fun, upbeat conversations. Like this week my cousin will tell all about her camping trip to Table Rock Lake in the Ozarks."

She goes to the foot reflexologist once a week, takes a digestive enzyme each meal and drives to another chiropractor just across the Missouri border, whom I've heard does nutritional kinesiology and cell-strength testing.

About growing old, she says, "One day you look in the mirror and just don't recognize yourself." About how she came to be so confident? It was her father's trust in her, growing up on the farm. "He told me that I could drive a car when I could safely back the tractor out of the barn."

Hazel is my patient for all our years here, well into her nineties. She tells how in mid-winter she walks in her basement for exercise, how she volunteers weekly at the Presbyterian Home serving coffee to much younger residents. She used to go to my first chiropractor, Dr. Gretchen Schreffler, who practiced in Kalona for many years before moving to Iowa City. "I loved to see her in her red high heels and her white clinic dress," she laughs. Me too.

One day she confides, "I was sitting in church last Sunday, just like every other Sunday. I looked at the people in front of my pew and I became aware that my mind had frozen." Her gray eyes look at me in quiet seriousness. "And I realized suddenly that I could not remember anyone's name."

I hold my breath and my own thoughts.

"So I just sat there quietly for several long minutes. Then it all came back to me." She smiles. I smile and squeeze her rangy hand.

If a person tests weak to the statement, "I am who I want to be in my Life," then who is he? Many are "who others want or need me to be."

Inferring What Some People Think

In this neighborhood, we've had to put our own tin flip-door mailbox out on the wooden shelf that holds the varied assortment of our neighbors' mail receptacles. There are probably ten or twelve boxes in various colors and stages of oxidative stress out there on the opposite corner from our house. Ours is new and shiny, quart-sized instead of pint-sized for our personal and professional mail, with just one small dent where the mail truck clipped it. A couple weeks ago we received an invitation to some Lavender Dance up in the City — a piece of queer mail with no brown envelope like we asked, which Tess's List said they would provide.

MARGARET: *Look here we got some letter from Kit Turner of Iowa City.*

KAREN: *Well open it and see what it is. It's probably an apology for screwing up and sending us stuff without the plain brown wrapper.*

MARGARET: *Well, it's a response all right but it's definitely not that. Get this. She's telling us what low self-esteem we must have for wanting our mail delivered that way. "I'm sorry for your inability to be forthright and hold your head high in your community as out lesbians."*

KAREN: *Oh my god, is she serious? This is small-town Iowa. I don't need to flaunt my private life in their faces. Let's get off that list immediately.*

Since our home practice is located in the middle of the town, only a block over and three up the hill from Chester's house (which he is now living in with his new wife Myrtle, who, bless her heart, took him in for his elder days) we are in the thick of it. The house looks pretty good as people drive by or when they swarm to their favorite shady seats in our yard, along the Fourth of July Parade route, to watch the high school marching band, the cheer squad, the fire trucks, local politicians, old guys on their antique tractors, a few horses or mules and local businesses throwing candy. One year there was even a brand-new, bright-green, giant hog-sewage-spreading machine.

Before we opened, Karen sanded and stained the woodwork in the entryway and stairwell, including the three mini-windows, their sills thigh-high when you step up along the staircase that peers out on Main Street. The upper panes have glass borders of rose-pink, sleepy-blue and soft golden-yellow stained glass. They are part of the original house charm, creating a placid glow in the afternoon sun, altering flat gray winter light to creamy pastel. Their location also means that we do no vacuuming of the steps in the nude.

We've come to know, only by conjecture and extrapolation, what some townspeople think of us being here. Our immediate neighbor up Main Street is the town osteopath, son of Doc Graber, the original medical doctor and his snooty wife, Velma. We first meet her out front as she walks past to visit her son. She says something like, "Well, I'm sure you know who *we* are."

Causing me to think, *And I'm sure you think you know who we are.* I don't take her personally, though. Most likely she talks to any newcomer in that uppity way.

One gloomy, early-spring Saturday afternoon, the doorbell rings. I gallop down the steps from my upstairs worktable and there is a woman my age, in jeans and a shirt knotted at the waist, with a clipboard in her hand. I recognize her broad, tenacious face from years ago in Iowa City when she was involved in anti-Vietnam War resistance and the flowering of feminist politics. Then, I remember that she is also our neighbor, the osteopath's, sister. I search my mind's rolodex, only finding distant fuzzy film clips as I open the door.

"Wow," she exclaims, before any polite greeting. "What are *you* doing here?"

"Well," I laugh, "That's a long story. What are you doing back here?"

She stammers a bit and blinks to protect herself from really seeing. "It's a project for a master's degree. Interviewing older residents of the town about … But, what are you …?" Her side of the conversation fades.

I say that we've opened a chiropractic practice here and watch her face explode in startled disbelief. "Would you like to come in for … "

She rushes to blurt, "Uh, well I've got to, uh, go." She backs down the porch steps wearing a cross-angled smile before turning to flee.

I stand pondering the encounter, imagining a collision of cultures, past and present — the romantic, warped, small-town past unable to hide from the incursion of worldly truths or whatever fearful tide of otherness that we might represent. We will now be out-ed with certainty to the osteopath, his wife, the nurse and her circle, their son, the possible junior-high bully, and Doc Graber and Velma. It was bound to happen. Clearly the sensitivities of the past are not yet healed. They seem to have begun lapping up to our doorstep.

"Who was that?" asks Karen, as she grumps down the steps, disturbed from an afternoon snooze.

"That was Lynda Graber. You know, our neighbor's sister? Another of the gracious children of old Doc Graber. She's a feminist from Iowa City. I guess she's just experienced her worlds colliding."

"Does she appear in that long, tortuous story of your early-'70s feminist, coming-out days … right about the time in the recounting where I always fall asleep?"

"Not really. We met through my old friend Day-Day … they were both into politics in ways I wasn't. I did hear a story that she and Franny Hornbaum got drunk and drove her VW bug all over the Wellman golf course. She seemed pretty freaked out to see us here. Perhaps we are wrecking her tidy reconciliation with the past. She certainly didn't offer any insights into the community or suggestion about … well, anything at all."

The encounter with Lynda seems oblique and only allows speculation about what people might be thinking. A better indication of putative background gossip comes from a series of encounters with young boys. I imagine they think themselves pretty clever. The first occurs on a weekend afternoon when I am carrying groceries up the front steps from the open hatch of the car. A grade-school boy in a flapping oversized T-shirt and shorts comes pedaling by on his BMX bike. Cheeks aglow, hair flying, he is grinning and shrieking, "What's your phone number? My sister wants to know."

When we get our first answering machine, there are August afternoons when summer activities have ended and the boredom level is spiking before the start of middle school. We receive several recorded messages offering us the self-promotion and certainty of sexual satisfaction that only a thirteen-year-old boy can pro-vide, followed by gales of laughter. Including ours — as long as we don't inadvertently play one of these ardent offerings in front of a patient. These we report to the phone company. Somehow they seem to know their origin and the proffers stop immediately.

One fall afternoon, after the last patient has left for the day, I am out front sweeping leaves off the side-walk. Another kid hurtles his bike down Main Street. He is going fast enough to avoid recognition, yet yowl-ing an elongated shriek into the wind, "Ar-ti-fi-cial in-sem-in-a-tion!" OK, evidence is amassing.

I later discover that even some of the older boys, possibly not indifferent, participate from a covert dis-tance. As I walk the dogs each night, conversing with the moon and stars and my arboreal friends along the old graying, tree-lined sidewalks, occasionally a dark sedan with a couple of churlish teenagers skulks along the quiet streets at a distance. Through an open window a voice croons, "Dyyyyke." I tell the dogs to ignore them. But I think to myself that these boys are too old to just be mimicking their parents' prejudices. Isn't this a bit too much interest?

Together these events let us know that we and gayness are specific topics of conversation — maybe disrespectful, dismissive ones, maybe ones with emotional impact, certainly of a sort to activate puerile imaginations.

Our patients do not care. The older ones may not notice or care to think of it. One old Amish man visiting from another community asks if we are sisters and, in the same breath, asks us to join him and his family at church. Those our age or younger are Shiloh Californians or simply beyond prejudice and see us for who we are and what we can do for them.

It amazes me what people's Bodies will say: I am strong and confident, yet simultaneously, I do not think I am strong and confident.

Creation Story

KAREN: *I have to do insurances tomorrow.*

MARGARET: *OK. I'll steer clear. Anything I can do to ease your pain?*

KAREN: *I can't really talk about the subject.*

MARGARET: *Well ... how about a new puppy?*

Karen plops the foot-high stack of manila folders on the kitchen table, away from the place settings. We each ignore them since insurance is a contentious subject. Its very mention triggers the obnoxious mountain of truth that she knows way more intimately than I, since many of her patients have Medicare or chiropractic insurance for a skeletal coverage of her involved care; and my care is not covered or even contemplated, since it doesn't fit the program.

The process of filling out a single page of patient visits is designed to be a complicated to-do, with many tricky little meaningless boxes, to offset the reality that chiropractors have mainly four codes to use depending on how many areas of the spine we adjust. Meanwhile, adjusting a sphenoid cranial bone, the talus of the foot, or even a rib is either ignored or put into an undifferentiated extremity category. So data accumulated on our services is overly simplistic or nonexistent. There is no knowledge of how the patient was instructed about her shoes, her pillow, his truck seat or his digestive enzyme, or kinesiotaped and given reflex points to restore the structure of the joint. The trick is the damn little boxes, which will invariably cause one or several rejections. This translates to delay in reimbursement to the patient of their now definitely-not-enough thirty-five-dollar fee and insults their credible expectations. They do not understand that there will be no way to reach a company spokesperson to explain the deliberate stall tactics. They will get perturbed with Karen and she will have to tell them that it's their contract and they will have to deal with their own representative. So I'm already planning to be out of the house tomorrow when I see her head for the kitchen.

We sit down to dinner. Franny, the ten-pound, long-haired miniature dachshund with a sleek dark coat and red feather-like wisps, and Millie, the seventy-five-pound Shepherd/wolf, are curled up on the sheepskin beneath the heavily scarred pine table, their compatible natures indifferent to their sizes.

Karen's soft, green oxford shirt, with sleeves rolled to the elbow, matches her eyes and sets off her cap of blonde hair. She mutters about the insurance thing, how different it is from actually doing the work. "Remember, I had that sensation of how it would feel to do this work before I ever came to Palmer? Remember? I told you that story," she says.

I do sort of remember, but prompt her to remind me again just because it's fun to retell our creation myths over time. "I remember the chiropractor guy who looked like Albert Einstein, who charged you six dollars and got rid of your migraines."

"Yes, he put me on my side and thunked my atlas vertebra. My great lady-scientist brain was startled."

I interject briefly from the annals of chiropractic, "Besides getting blood to that very brain."

"Yes, there's that. It made me have to rethink everything. *Now Karen, examine this new arena of data.* That was a big step for a university-trained scientist." Then, over lasagna and mixed green salad with cheese from some nice rich goat, she retells the story.

One Saturday Seattle morning, she awakens and finds herself in two places. She's lying snuggly in bed. At the same time, she is alert and standing in a formal room talking to an imposing middle-aged guy with smooth black hair, wearing a white suit. She quickly emphasizes that this is not some woo-woo angel in flowing robes or anything. I think of B.J. Palmer himself, come back from the astral plane to recruit her.

As though on assignment to deliver a telegram of importance, this interdimensional being announces, "You are going to be a chiropractor."

She counters immediately, "That is a completely ridiculous statement. Outlandish actually. I already have a job. I have a career as a senior oceanographer … plus a mortgage to pay."

Then Dr. WhiteSuit bargains with her. "OK, here's what we are going to do. For one week, I am going to allow you to feel how you are going to feel if you become a chiropractor. Then you've got a year to wrap up your research and get enrolled."

She winces at that. Then, just as quickly, he vanishes. She is fully back in bed, also fully awake. Maybe a bit cracked open at the conversation. After wondering for a long moment if this is a breakdown (Should she admit herself to the psych ward?) she decides to continue on with the day as normally as possible.

Rolling out of bed, she puts on a thick maritime sweater and dark-blue corduroys. She drives her little tan Toyota pickup toward Puget Sound and pulls into a parking garage by the farmer's market. In the soothing morning mist she walks aimlessly among the mingling aromas of cinnamony Swedish baked goods and the catch of the day. Even in the crush and jostle of Saturday shoppers, with their bulky bags of produce and blazing flowers, she feels quiet and content. *I feel as though I am doing something very worthwhile. There is this huge helmet of energy around my head. My hands are pulsing and seem enormous.*

The sensation lasts a full week. Karen feels great and begins to get comfortable with inner buoyancy. Then, at the end of the week, it departs in a collapsing thud. She realizes how depressed she is. How disgusted she is with the infighting and posturing in her once-esteemed field.

She begins wrapping up her affairs. But then, as the ego does in moments of change and loss, she begins to lose her identity and becomes anxious and drifts away from the newfound plan. Then WHAM! She is rear-ended in her truck and once again needs to visit the chiropractor. In a few visits he eases the blow to her cervical spine. In that moment she realizes she could do this for people. The focus of her commitment returns; wrap-up continues.

Even so, her anxiety comes back so she takes her friend's recommendation and goes to a Gestalt therapist. While talking to a pillow in a chair, she begins to communicate with the parts of her disintegrating personality: The severe clipboard lady in black menaces her with worry and fear of the unfamiliar; the soft-spoken intuitive little girl in flowing colorful clothes takes a stand, "If you don't let me go, I will make your life miserable;" and the fix-it guy, the young man in coveralls carrying a hammer, grins confidently, saying it will be just fine.

Discovery of this complex depth of self and deep dialogue gives her a fresh understanding and sense of reassurance. But this is new, not her accustomed practice of thinking, always thinking. Her current job is observing, counting, thinking, comparing, analyzing. Once again the old habit takes over. She begins to think *How is it that I can just leap into the unknown? I know nothing about this new way to be. Plus, there's more school. Even if I've begun studying psychic phenomenon and have science fiction experience, how can I trust this? Perhaps if I give what I'm doing one more try ...*

She wavers once more. Then WHAM again! The little Toyota pickup gets rear-ended once more. She crawls out from behind the wheel and cries, "All right. All right, I'm going."

She does not look back.

Pushed back from the table now, she looks at the files with a mixture of pride and loathing. They have accumulated for quite some time and really must be attended to. "At least I have that good feeling most days."

Balancing a person who is making a huge life change can be informed by muscle testing the person metaphorically standing at a threshold, entering a new life, leaving an old life behind, then finding out what they need to be strong.

Landon

MARGARET: *I got you some co-op tiramisu. Want a little? Did you see The Wellman Advance this week? They've published the amounts of the subsidies to the farms in our area.*

KAREN: *Sure. Here you can use this plate. ... By name?*

MARGARET: *Last year it was by names of individuals, but this year it's by farm names instead. Maybe there was blowback when everyone got to see how much money was involved.*

KAREN: *How much?*

MARGARET: *Well, it seems deliberately unclear. Last year they were listed as the husband, the brother, the wife and/or the son, and they each got amounts from $40,000 to $60,000. This year it's listed by farm names, so it's more difficult to tell. Seems like a big farm could harvest a million or more taxpayer dollars every ten years. Don't you imagine that's how the big farms have the resources to buy up the smaller farms?*

KAREN: *Probably. Can't think about that now ... Mmm, this is good.*

I walk Landon upstairs, passing our reflections in the pastel-bordered windows, to my treatment room. He sits, leaning forward in the patient chair across from me with a handsomeness that he seems to spend rather than own. He wears black fitted jeans and a checked shirt and looks to me more like a guy in a Seattle coffee shop than a farmer. His brown eyes seem bright and open and, at the same time, concealing. The intake form says he is just a few months older than I am.

"I need to get my energy back after this bout of chemo," he says. "My wife thinks acupuncture might help."

He lies on my treatment table. Fine silver needles poke from his pale torso and wrists. A bolster supports his bare white legs with needles below his knees and near his ankles in the peppery sprinkle of dark hairs. As he lies there, I wonder, does he lie? Maybe. The idea creeps in from the periphery. Why do I think this? His conversation seems ordinary. "The oats are sown," he says. "They start in late winter, early spring. After a little more heat to dry the fields, we'll get in the corn..." Simple talk. Do I hear a poor-me sort of tone? Is there another subliminal motive besides the farm report?

Our ages being nearly the same, I'm reminded of boys from high school, then of letter sweaters and box-pleated skirts, cars — all that cool stuff that turned out to be nostalgic crap from a time of learning to be "just a girl."

Let's see. In home ec, I learned to make white sauce and set the table for my future husband and listened to my teacher tell me, "You shouldn't carry your books on your hip like that. It's not ladylike." In English, there was one exceptional teacher, Mr. Hanlon, who did his best to repair the damage of the putrid teacher who everlastingly licked his dry lips, just waiting for his after-school barstool, sneering that women are feeble sentimentalist writers. Mr. Hanlon was kind, smart and funny even if he had a crew cut with a widow's peak and an unfortunate smile with an underbite. He had us write two papers — *Man Is Basically Good* and *Man Is Basically Evil.* I couldn't figure out the argument for the second one and had to ask. Turns out it was because of needing to be saved by Jesus' crucifixion. Very embarrassing and, at the same time, refreshing that as a supposed Lutheran kid, I didn't know that.

There were only boys in chemistry, which was required before taking advanced biology — which never even got taught, probably because the teacher was a woman with dated 1940s' hair rolls. By the time my guidance counselor droned out my aptitude and college prep results, adding, as though by accident, that students with my scores most likely go on to get postgraduate degrees, he might have been pulling a piece of lint off his sleeve. It took some years for me to figure out that the boys got actual guidance and career networking.

Now, from my chair, I notice that Landon's post-chemo curly dark hair weeps into colorless shades at his temples, and I realize that he has been talking about some sculpted thing he's making, and is now onto, "... so I really appreciate our fathers and admire the 'greatest generation.'"

"Do you now?" I say as if I've been on this journey with him all along. "I'm not sure that I feel the same."

"Oh, but it's true ..." he continues as my mind can't quite fathom his opinion since that superlative gives our generation no option but to be "less than." I silently think that Karen and I have spent our lives generally ignored or insulted by the greatest generation … much more favorable for Landon, I imagine. But what is it I perceive here? Perhaps he's a thwarted artist, unable to conceive of such a life what with all that has been gifted upon him.

"So," I say, "let's take these needles out for today. Shall we meet again next week?"

He looks stronger and reveals more with each subsequent visit. "This week I'm feeling much better, like I'm going to be able to get the rest of the spring planting done. My wife's Golden Retriever bitch had her litter. The puppies are fun, especially now that the kids are mostly out of the house and into their own lives." He sounds sweet and nice, yet superficial. There's a gaping emotional hole somewhere and I feel he's not telling all. Nothing about how he felt having cancer in his testicle, for example, or seeing that in a broader context. The picture to the outside world is rosy with his unaffected, competent wife, virtuous children, the farm legacy from his greatest-generation dad and, now, new puppies.

As his strength returns to normal, he begins to reek of corporatist agriculture from behind his hip fashion and nice-guy veneer. It seeps from him like the scent of an illicit affair. He describes his Ag school education in Ames with a pride tantamount to acting on Broadway or voyaging with Greenpeace. He doesn't explicitly mention being strapped to his university desk while an artificially sweetened elixir of select science is drizzled down his gullet. Apparently there's only phantom memory of that tantalizing, propagandizing dominatrix sliding her tongue along the spirals of his ear, plunging deep and close to his brain, whispering *Subsidies*.

I'd like to like him. Theoretically he's in my grade; me from a graduating class of 650 and he from one of maybe sixty-five. Plus, now that he has responded well to his acupuncture, I want to tell him some stories from the other world, albeit an unsubsidized one — stories that go along with how we care for our patients — that I've learned at the annual Upper Midwest Organic Growers Conference in Wisconsin. Like the one told by the seventy-five-year-old veterinarian taking care of market hogs in the fifties ... he's a "greatest generational."

As a young doc, he'd been puzzling over a certain pig farm run by two brothers. Each spring he went out to their place to vaccinate and castrate swine, but then he didn't hear from them all year until the following spring. Why didn't they call him for farrowing or sick-piggy-care the rest of the year? By the third spring, he got up enough courage to ask them if they preferred someone else's care during the rest of the year. The brother's looked at him quizzically, then realized his predicament. "It's not that we don't like you, Doc. We just don't have sick pigs. We grow our own feed, have plenty of open pasture, plus you don't see any empty pesticide containers on our land. We don't call you because we don't need you."

I dare to share with Landon bits about other organic farmers, their crop rotation schedules, their pasture-raised animals and minimal-inputs farming, each creating the best products from their specific micro-climate. I tell him because he's the one recovering from cancer, but his unconcerned eyes and languid body are not listening. He's the "next generation." How can he not know best? "In farming, now, we have to seriously consider our responsibility to feed the world," he says.

I know. I know. I hear that theme repeated again and again. It's a corporate argument served up along with a free pork sandwich and new feed cap. It has nothing to do with feeding us — their fellow citizens — or preserving the land, our water, our health. It is part of a continued push to export more and more grain and livestock to Japan, China and wherever, supported by the taxpayers. Landon doesn't question the indus-trial farm or his certainty of its promising future, even if it is soaked with toxic chemicals, genetically altered seeds and government obligation. He's smug. There's that scent again.

Today is his last treatment. After a month and a half, he's pretty much recovered his strength. "I do feel better," he says, tucking in his shirttails.

"I'm glad," I say, shaking his warm hand. "I imag-ine you'll get stronger and stronger."

He walks down the porch steps, back into his acco-laded world. I guess I just feel glum. At his squandered potential. At the vast consequences of his choices.

And then, in a confluence of thought, I remember another patient, some months ago, a woman confiding that she'd spent long, wistful hours on the phone each week talking to a guy she was having some sort of liaison with. I remember the name she inadvertently shared — Landon.

According to muscle testing, it turns out it's possible for a person to believe two equal and opposite things at the same time like, "I love mySelf; I hate mySelf."

Crimes, Misdeeds, Villainy and a Few Simple Mistakes

MARGARET: *I heard that the town is thinking about moving its money to one of these new State of Iowa savings accounts with higher interest rates.*

KAREN: *Well it's the talk of the town that old Mr. Khaki, Gordon the banker, was at the most recent town council meeting. He was questioned about the one million dollars that Wellman keeps in an account in Wellman Savings Bank. And guess what? It just sits there making no interest.*

MARGARET: *Wow! What an arrogant ... What's the council going to do? Transfer the money? How does that affect the council members? And the mayor? The mayor owns that gas station right downtown, pathetic as it is. And Julie Kincade's furniture store is the last big business in town except the Ford and Chevy dealers ... well, and the cement plant. Always need cement, especially with the new hog factories.*

KAREN: *When I was in Kincade's Furniture she told me that Gordon is threatening to not loan money to her customers for buying furniture if the council insists that the bank pay interest. And he's already pulled Mayor Helmuth's loan. His station will have to close.*

It's a humid, hot summer Saturday afternoon. We are wrapping up after a day of fixing, mowing, dusting and cleaning so we can take our aging dogs for a late-evening walk, when it cools a bit. Karen is finishing up in the kitchen. I've been in our oblong backyard, in my side-pocket work shorts and a skimpy T-shirt, thanklessly trimming back Medusa-like tree of heaven shoots along the fence adjacent the neighbor to the east.

I'm also admiring the sturdiness of the little deck I built off the mudroom door. It's only about seven feet deep because that's how far the garage extends beyond the house. It snugs up next to the garage, skims over the original old hand-dug well with a rotting wooden cover, surrounds a ten-inch diameter mulberry tree which will drop purple berries and stain the deck but make me and the birds very happy and extends toward the front of the house four feet beyond the back door, where the yard begins its gentle slope toward the street. In the twelve-inch space underneath the front side both Millie and Franny are snoozing on cool dirt in the afternoon heat.

The little crank-out window of Karen's downstairs bath and shower room is next to the mudroom. Now that the Medusa tree has grown up a bit, it makes it more difficult for the nosy, unpleasant (lots of our patients say so) old man next door to see in when he suddenly needs to drink his morning coffee in his otherwise-empty side yard.

I'm ready to come in when Karen sticks a perspiring arm out the back door, holding a blue plastic bucket partly full of some leftover cleaning liquid. "Hey honey, will you empty this?"

"Sure," I say, as she disappears back inside. I take the bucket beyond the deck not far from the house and pitch it onto a patch of moist sparse grass. Instantly, silently shrieking earthworms surge out of the ground, stretching their mucousy bodies out to eight inches long to try to escape whatever noxious thing I have just poured over them. It startles me like an astral firecracker exploding — soft, squishy worm bodies flinging themselves in agony away from the liquid.

I rush inside to fill the bucket with clear water to dilute my aggression. "What was in that?" I cry to Karen.

"Oh, just some bleach I was using."

Rushing out, I say, "Well our worms are aggrieved. And you can't believe how many are under a square foot of earth." I pour the clear water over them and pick up eight or ten to rinse and toss to shaded safety.

We gather the dogs. Millie, the shepherd wolfdog, has a benign name, after the former first dog of George H.W. Bush. That's so people will be unafraid of her — as opposed to T-Rex or Killer. But with Franny, the dachshund who's approximately one-eighth her size and takes six steps and three waddles to every one of hers, they are mostly just incongruous and amusing. We head out the garage door and on up the hill to Thirteenth Street. Millie and I are ahead, Karen and Franny behind. At the top of the hill, in the lazy warm evening, we step into the street, side by side for the three blocks to the entrance into North Park.

We talk about how Karen has been the one to deal with the next set of bankers — this time from a Washington bank since we are ready to buy the house outright from the owners. "They send these three guys

— Williams, Beanblossom and Turnipseed," she says. "Too bad they aren't as lighthearted and comical as their names. They harrumph about in this self-important, old-guy manner. Everything looks great and yet they cannot find us *girls* solvent enough to let us assume the mortgage. So we'll have to buy it on contract. I was thinking bad thoughts about the arrogant small-town pricks."

As we stroll, the dogs are immune to life among humans. They linger occasionally to read the neighborhood news, sniffing and snuffling, intermittently commenting and making their own statements by peeing and marking the bushes. In the park, we pass the two baseball diamonds, the sturdy picnic shelter, a new sand volleyball court, the kids' colorful, curvy playground equipment and the old band shell that looks like a cement quarter of a grapefruit.

I don't know what to say, except it's tiresome and predictable.

Just beyond the playground equipment we walk into a humid, acrid gust of hog stink. Now I know what to say, "Oh god, is that awful! That's probably from Clyde Olmstead's new pig factory farm just north of here." The smell disperses a bit as we move on down toward the golf course.

There's more in the week's gossip mill that Karen has learned from her patients. Julie Kincade and her husband are moving their counties-wide popular furniture and mattress store to Kalona because of the banker.

"And why did the bank let that Lydie woman open her western clothing store in the empty storefront next to Kincade's?" I ask, as we walk in the exuberant green grass. "I went in there before she went out of business. Who would fund such a business plan these days? Just cutesy girls' clothes and expensive women's jeans — no tack or feed. Doomed to failure competing with the big box stores."

"It's because her collateral was that sweet little horse property, southwest of town out beyond Foster Woods Park, that she and her husband owned. The tragedy of how she did not lose the property when the business went bust is because of the insurance policy on her not quite ex-husband when he plowed into their gate post driving blind drunk and was killed outright."

"What a thief that banker is! And Chester used to be so proud of his stepson who works for him. See we didn't have enough to lose. And were too likely not to lose it. That's why he didn't loan you any money."

"I know. I've had my account there for these few years and, now that it's amounting to something," Karen boasts, "I'm going to move it to Hills Bank in Kalona, where yours is. Maybe he'll holler at me too. My patient Carol Olson told me he followed old Mildred Owens out of the bank the other day screaming at her out on the sidewalk that she was not a true Wellmanite. Apparently as soon as her husband passed, she went in and closed all their accounts and moved them to Washington."

"So now Larry Helmuth has lost his gas station, the Kincades are gone and the Lydie place is bust. Our tax base is heading for the toilet. You'd think it'd be time for us to be going, but your popularity is growing and even mine is gaining momentum, thanks to my Iowa City referral hubs."

We come to the end of the park and scuttle down a short hill, cut through the elementary school's playground and cross the yard of the Wellman Historical Society's little one-room Smith Creek School. Two blocks later we're coming up the sidewalk to the front of our house. Dogs' tongues are hanging low in the warm humid evening. We're going in for some fresh gazpacho and quesadillas.

"Hey, what's this?" I say. There's a flimsy envelope stuck in our wooden screen door. "Here, see what this is and I'll take the dogs in." I pass Karen the envelope.

Inside our shade-sheltered house it's still cool. The dogs sit and get their leashes removed, then head for the food and water bowls. They chomp and gobble their respective treats.

Karen comes into the kitchen with a crushed envelope in one hand and holding a piece of lined tablet paper in the other. "Get this," she says. "You know how I arranged for that young Mennonite woman to come in and clean our house once a week? And she was going to start next Tuesday?"

"I know, how great... was?" I say.

"Yeah. Was. It seems that she has written to say she is unable to work for us because of our lifestyle. Even though last Tuesday when we went over the chores around the house, there seemed to be no problem."

"And after she's been in to scope out our house. Maybe she's related to one of those Washington bankers. What's her last name? Cabbageleaf? I had no idea lesbian money was so unacceptable. Did you? I wonder if your patients know this is how their neighbors behave?"

Dinner is fresh but its savoriness has dulled. Later on, upstairs, we crack the windows before crawling into bed, hoping for a bit of cooling night relief. After a short goodnight kiss of solidarity, we sigh, squeeze hands and lay our heads close on our separate pillows. Then, *Oh my god, what is that smell?* A plume of reeking stench from that hog lagoon has resumed tainting our cooling night breeze.

One of us says, "I don't care how hot it is up here, we've got to close these windows."

"Fuck, what a day," says the other.

After letting the Truth be True and discovering what the subconscious has come to believe that does not suit the evolving Self, the Balance begins as we retune the Body to something affirming.

Pickup Soliloquy

Karen gets up in the middle of the night.

KAREN: *Oh no!*

MARGARET: *What is it?*

KAREN: *It's a bat in the bathroom!*

MARGARET: *OK (mumbling herself awake). I'm coming.*

A palm-sized leathery gray creature clings to the wall over the bathtub. Margaret, in a blue T-shirt, slips down the stairwell and back to grab the broom from near the front door. She opens the bathroom's folding window as far as it goes, pries the screen out of its wooden frame, pulls back the shower curtain and steers the little flapping mammal out of the corner, watching as it flies out the window.

KAREN: *OK. I'm ready ... What are you doing?*

MARGARET: *Just putting the screen back.*

KAREN: *You mean it's out? Look at you! Weren't you worried? I had to put on a raincoat, hood and boots.*

Tonight I'm going to take the back roads to the tiny campground at Lake Darling at the southern end of the county. It's an August night in 1998; the Perseid meteor shower is coming on.

Time to head out. Let's see, I have on a long-sleeved Tee, cute side-pocket shorts and Chaco sandals, which means my furry legs are out in the breeze. I go through the garage, carrying a hamper with fragrant potato salad — no dill, anise seeds instead. Plus, the ingredients for tomorrow's breakfast and the Dalai Lama's new book *The Art of Happiness*. The others are already at the campground — Karen and our friends, Rayleen and Roxanne (Ray and Rox), veterinarians from a small town near the park. Plus, Millie and our new young corgi named Murphy. Most likely beer bottles are open and steaks with peppers and onions sizzle on the grill. I worked late for a Friday. The forty-minute drive will give me some time alone to process the overwhelm that's in my head.

Our patients tell all. So, even without TV, we've been deluged with the embarrassments of President Bill Clinton. A lawsuit from an aggrieved woman and a current liaison with 20-something-year-old White House aide. Endless denials from the first president of my own age. The one who also said he didn't inhale — who believes that?

I turn the ancient handle of the wooden-plank garage door, pushing it open with a mini roar as it suspends overhead. The old fir boards have the reassuring 100-year-old smell of stability opening to the warm end of daylight on this late-summer day. The garage is my place of childhood mythical adventure. I still hear my mother say, "Get that mess out of the house and play with it in the garage." It's a place of contemplation and philosophizing here on the bench next to my Bucket Boss of hand tools, my new Japanese saws and a few gardening implements by the dusty window. It's where I conquered my perfectionistic procrastination with my triumphant "15-Minute Solution." Five minutes to assess the job — a latch, a stuck closet door, a loose board on the deck. Five minutes to get the necessary tools. Five minutes to fix it. Most liberating.

The summer's dusk surrounds me. I look out on the street in our little, supposedly nothin' town where many kind, gentle people nestle in their homes. They're not that far from less gentle houses where children hide from their fathers, uncles and occasionally their injurious mothers and live in desperate circumstances. I learn something about these lives in the Balance room.

I also discover that each person seems to live on two tracts. One is an inner Self that is all the time evolving in its revelations of awareness. It needs to be wooed, coaxed and unconditionally supported — not overrun by a false self, created by external culture that equates competence with beauty and money. A fearful barrage of dystopian malaise and competitiveness doesn't help people learn kindness or compassion. I think about what great things happen in our treatment rooms. It feels glorious to help people with means they don't even know exist. And why should they? It's our job.

I gather my parcels and walk out into the dusky evening. After I lower the white-painted garage door and put the hamper in the passenger seat of Karen's maroon pickup with the **PARODOX** license plates, I climb into the driver's seat. A glance at the rearview mirror shows the totem hanging from it — a little square of soft suede with turquoise glass beads around a tiny ceramic Our Lady of Guadalupe.

Beyond the edge of town, I flick the radio knob and it's suddenly 1980 again. Donna Summer singing "On the Radio." I disco along the skinny road, with its mown shoulders, between hulking cornfields. My left foot taps the dashboard as I dance along with the song, past the Schroeder farms down the road from each other. I've loved airwave synchronistic messages since listening under the covers to my crystal radio as a kid.

Once in high school, on the way to a big debate contest, my friend's dad had the radio on. Attorney General Bobby Kennedy was speaking. Suddenly I realized he was talking about our debate topic. He was clinching the argument for one side of the question! *Oh no!* I thought. *What should I do?*

Anymore, I don't remember the debate question — something regarding U.S. policy in South America — maybe the Alliance for Progress. I was just a fill-in, inflating the team for the big contest. Which means I spent a couple afternoons preparing with the admirable varsity debaters to deliver the goods at the tournament. But hearing these remarks on the radio gave me pause. I copied the quote on a file card with "not" in brackets — preparing to read it either way depending on which side I was arguing. It turned out I didn't need to use the "not" and misquote him, but I would have, intending to win either way.

In college, later on in the sixties, I listened to late-night Beaker Street from the 50,000-watt station KAAY in Little Rock, Arkansas. Filling the lonely after-midnight frequencies with psychedelic music and excerpts from The Firesign Theatre. And that interview with Ayn Rand one night. In her gritty Russian accent, she said, "Each man must live as an end in himself." That one sentence caused me to question any tiny flake of altruistic inclination. Fortunately, I later retrieved my sensibility and understood it as my search for compassion.

Now, here's the T intersection where I turn left, the light from my headlights spotlighting the cornrows. Then a meteor shoots right across the horizon in front of me. *Make a wish!* It's a glimpse from the outer realms. Then, speaking of very old radio, I remember Karen singing from Big Jon and Sparkie:

A shooting star is not a star; it's not a star at all.
A shooting star's a meteorite that's headed for a fall.

I punch a different station. Here's NPR on the hour, news time. I hear President Bill's voice, his choking Arkansas accent, "I did have an inappropriate relationship with…" Oh no, Oh no. After all his parsing, lying, scapegoating. Oh no. This is not high school debate; this is the fucking presidency, man. Don't do this stuff, and don't lie. You become so weak. I'm crying and yelling at the now immovable stars. What a lousy disappointment.

He finishes his stunning remarks and I punch the radio buttons again in frustration. Here's an ad for a popular fungicide, probably on these fields all around me. And then, what else? Steel guitar and the crescen-do of Tammy Wynette singing "Stand By Your Man." I guess that's for you Hillary. I punch another button and it's the melodic mouthsmart Dixie Chicks taking us out with "There's Your Trouble." "Shoulda been different but it wasn't different..." Enough. I spin the knob off.

Night softness covers the last twenty minutes of the drive. There are few valleys along this once-open, marshy, deep-grass prairie, now evermore fields with straight country roads to the horizon. Three more well-spaced right turns and here's the sign to Lake Darling. I slow onto the smooth macadam, into the park lawns and cooling fresh of creeks and big oak trees. These old woods at the edge of harm have some remaining ease. There are a few boats moored along the quarter-mile lake. On around the curve, many camping spaces are occupied with vehicles, tents and campers among the smoky scents of evening campfires. I turn onto a gravel bed next to our little camper. Four lawn chairs hold three sets of bare legs and sneakers stretched out before the fire. Three bright smiles of welcome. Simul-taneously, three voices:

"Hey you made it! Did you bring the potato salad?"

"We are deliberating the significance of the missing leg of the Y chromosome in the XY configuration and its effects on the survival of civilization."

"I'm showing off my new running shoes!"

Murphy lopes over, his little knuckle of a tail wagging.

"Hello girls, it's good to be here!"

We discover the best statements for a Balance goal by testing: "This is good for me," "This brings me Joy."

Our Angels Ginny and Peter

KAREN: *I guess they didn't have anyone to talk to about this before. But now that we're here ... Let's see there's Ginny and Peter ...*

MARGARET: *We should have predicted that one.*

KAREN: *I know. Then there's the chorus director's daughter, a PhD minister who won't be able to preach in her Methodist church.*

MARGARET: *And Betty who owns the bar and told Stephie, her daughter, that she should correspond with women prisoners ... For what? A dating connection? And then my hairdresser's seventy-five-year-old Mennonite father has just come out to his middle-aged son. Nothing to lose at that age, I guess.*

KAREN: *There's Coach and Bryan and some others peeking out from under the skirts of the Shiloh church. And, of course, our neighbor's son who has been swishing around since he was able to walk. They'll probably blame us.*

O K, Ginny, but here's the thing," I say, as Karen and I pull out chairs for the three of us around our kitchen table. "It's just not going to be what you are hoping it will be."

We are at the end of our workday and the western sun sends soft horizontal rays through the kitchen windows. I serve us each some chamomile tea in the cat cups and think back to when we first met Ginny — when she rode with us in the vanpool up to the university. She's not tall, is somewhat wiry and usually has a wide ready smile. Peter is tall and lean, with a ponytail of brunette, scraggly hair. They are both academics — she a librarian at the university and he a language professor at the community college. They are both kind. In fact, they are our angel benefactors, offering the $1,000 for a chiropractic table that the banker so snobbishly refused. We've been guests in their unfinished solar house out north of town. They have been guests at this table.

I set down my steaming cup to focus on the issue at hand, which is that Peter has just come out. "Ginny, I know he says it will be fine to stay living under the same roof you've shared for the last twenty-five years. He truly would like to do that for you. Just like he really tried to stay true to being in the closet for all those years. But that closet door is busted off its hinges now. There's no going back. He says he would preserve the relationship you used to have ... except, it's not possible."

And now Ginny sits in a bound-up huddle around her fragrant cup, a former nun wearing large red glasses that cannot fully hide overflowing tears. "But ... he says he wants to make it as good for me as possible." It's a voice not comfortable with the personal unknown, a librarian not used to this level of disorder.

Karen and I exchange glances, possibly both thinking of Peter — his long-limbed, easy effeminate manner. Catholic guilt now counterbalancing Catholic repression.

I push on, "Soon, it's likely you'll see that your former life is just not available for you any longer. Yes, you have your grown son in common, but there will be new faces around your house. And not only will they be male, very possibly they'll be young males, perhaps flamboyant young males with eye liner." She looks startled and gives Karen a look of disbelief.

I peer into my cup wishing now that it was beer. "At least it's what I have observed; when a person comes out, or is suddenly sexually autonomous, they're often attracted to the age group of their previous sexual freedom. I know it's difficult but I think you'll get through this better if you have your own space."

We finally wear the subject out. There's no more to discuss. Ginny stands and we each give her a melted hug. I'm sure she will grow a cloak of capability to wrap round her astounded self. It may be a while before Ginny allows herself to think that she's really not surprised at this turn of events.

A few weeks later I'm in the kitchen preparing a little supper. I hear Peter's voice. He has come in to see Karen to get adjusted. After a bit she walks out of her adjusting room, authoritatively pronouncing him "Rather misaligned from his new exercise regime." I step into the middle room to view our new gay Adonis.

"Of course, you've heard," he says to me with a feigned sheepish smile.

"I have," I say. "Your life has changed a bit I guess?" I wait to hear anything he might want to reveal.

"Well, yes it has. I have a whole new circle...and well..." He pauses, lightly swaying and appearing to have something on his mind. My mind arcs through a lively perimeter of images and gay borderland stories I've experienced or heard through time. Then he says, "Well, I really need a new haircut. I know you've said you've cut Karen's and your hair in the past, can you do that for me?"

And so I do. The next weekend he sits in our kitchen, all lights on, towel around his shoulders. I comb out his tangle of thin, unhappy hair. His hairline has receded, but there's wavy healthy hair at the crown. I ceremonially whack a lifetime of uncertainty away, buzz off the remainders and trim him a cute cap of flirtatious ends.

Over the next few months, Ginny seems to be moving on pretty well. Karen sees her occasionally to get adjusted and reports, "She has an apartment in a cute brick house near Iowa City's northside neighborhood. I think she's having a sexy relationship with some extroverted guy. She looks happy, although a bit dazed. And a bit miffed at me when she comes to get adjusted. Her memory is that I was the one to break it to her, not you. You manage to say stuff all the time that people remember as though I said it."

"I know that's what you say. Lucky me. Maybe it's because they are used to you giving them specific directives about their bodies."

Then, as we wrap up another day, she says, "And I meant to tell you about my last visit with Peter. At his first medical checkup since his coming out, he apparently reports having a bright red stool and is immediately prescribed a bunch of AIDS-related tests. This by the guy he's seen for the last decade. Then it turns out he remembers eating a bowl of beet borscht the previous day."

"Yeah, still a difficult subject all round."

A Body will reveal its inner truths, even its sexuality — but it's too sensitive a topic to ask without the person's awareness or permission.

The Auction

Karen sits on the waiting room couch, smoothing Rain-dance's silky, cream-colored fur. He's a Birman breed cat with powder-blue eyes, dusky points and white-tipped paws. I am playing a feather game with Willie Mays — our American shorthair, black-and-gray classic tabby with a target design on the side of his coat. These two, plus Zackie, the sedate gray Persian, make up the current cat dynasty.

MARGARET: *Chester's place is up for auction in a month or so. Think we should fix it up for a new office? Then we could have one more room for acupuncture or a massage roller table, closer to downtown, with all that sunlight.*

KAREN: *You know, when Rebecca the hairdresser is on the adjusting table, she brings her three-year-old daughter Chrissy who likes to play with Raindance. We leave the door open and Chrissy picks him up and hauls his soft, droopy body out to the opposite east windows. Then she hops and skips back into the adjusting room, giggling. He looks at her calmly and then bolts across the room and is back by the time she is.*

MARGARET: *That's adorable. These farm women who have never had indoor animals seem to enjoy ours. And you know we have that picture of Jane's seventy-five-year-old mom, Ruby, sitting on the adjusting table petting Zackie.*

KAREN: *My practice is right where I want it to be; suits me just fine. I don't need more room. And at this rate we'll be able to pay off the house fairly soon.*

I walk down Main Street on August twenty-third, the appointed day, then laugh out loud when I realize it's Chester's birthday. Optimistic old talker that he was. I remember he thought he might entice a Philippine woman to the states to marry him, before Myrtle took up his cause. Wanted me to help him write his letter of introduction. I looked at the picture she'd sent — young, smiling golden face — and wondered how desperate she was. "Chester," I told him, "you'll do fine, just remember to include your picture." He liked the one of himself in front of his twenty-foot woodpile at his other house, next to his vibrant garden. He knew what a strong and charming soul he was behind the thick glasses and rugged farm jacket, with his gnarly, accomplished hands.

Of course the only thing that can be done with that property of his is to auction it. When we rented it we couldn't use the larger front bedroom facing the street because drainage from up the hill had stagnated along the next-door neighbor's garage and allowed the footings to sink the front corner of the house about five inches lower than the rest. The bathroom and kitchen are original — what 1930s? At least there is indoor plumbing and a teeny basement space with water heater and sewer pipes. And of course my favorite — the garage made from the hardwood conquests of his past.

I turn right toward Ninth Avenue and the destination, a block away. There are already cars parked on this street for those gathered to watch the show.

This is my first time to openly defy Karen. I've disagreed with her in the past, since we often look at things from completely opposite viewpoints, but at least it's been along a similar trajectory. She dislikes that — especially in front of others. And about this purchase, she will worry what people think about us owning this dump. She doesn't need to expand her space since she only works out of one room and she has a good, growing patient base. I would like to expand to two rooms and not have my people climb the stairs. It was good to have had our house on public display in the sense it made us seem open and welcoming, but it's now 1998 and time to expand. Won't she like having our house be ours and not the public's?

I've been stuck thinking about this for two months now — ever since I glimpsed the Auction sign in the yard on my evening dog walk with Murphy. I've tried to let it go, tried to talk my way out of it, but here I am unshaken, unrepentant. I did remind Karen last night that it's happening today. Today, I just say I'm going. She says she really doesn't like the idea. I say I have to do it. And I don't remind her that if I succeed and get it, it will impact us both financially since I can't afford to buy it on my own. But it is a perfect location, perfect layout and perfect size — and no stairs for patients to negotiate.

I cross Ninth Avenue, now two houses away. People are strolling about the lawn in the late morning shade of the forty-year-old maple and ash trees in the front. It's the looky-loos checking it out, and maybe some potential buyers — thirty or so altogether plus dark-haired, mustachioed Auctioneer Col. Mike Yokum. His mother, Maxine, is one of our committed patients.

I plan to bid and deal with consequences later. I vow to not pay more than $19,000 for lot and buildings. Suddenly it occurs to me that I am most unprepared. I have been so focused on the idea I have done no research on prices, have not been to the bank to get our new banker's approval. I've never even bought anything at an auction — well once I paid a dollar for a tub of junk so I could get a garden hose.

I step onto the familiar grass yard. It feels like the guys hanging about might be elbowing each other and winking, but I do not have an ounce of energy to spare on them. I must concentrate, yet try to breathe and grok what's happening. I don't need a tour. I know what's in there. I'm ready. And within ten minutes we've begun. Mike's red face begins calling in the summer sunshine. Maybe they start at $10,000, I don't quite remember. *Meeney, meeny, meeny, hah, mumble, mumble*; keening, pleading. I am unmoved. I wait. I watch closely.

There are several bids at first. Some banter. I wait a while longer. We take a break; maybe it's auctioneering psychology. They resume and I make my first bid. It's quickly countered. I bid again. It's countered. It seems like two of them. Are they interested or just pushing me? I bid. It's countered. We're getting up above $17,000. I step back a bit and let go. More *meeny mumble*. Mike takes another break. I walk around back and see the square plops of concrete making an ineffective sidewalk. I see the drafty aluminum windows, the curling roof shingles, the excellent southern exposure for beautiful light, the sturdy structure.

I refuse the pink punch glop. I do not think what Karen may be thinking. I am all in here. But things have changed a lot since the early days of our insulting bankers. Now we have Mindy, educated mother of three, vice-president to Alan, the new Swedish-looking president. They both have great faith in our fiscal trustworthiness.

Mike calls us back. I begin raising in small increments. Then *Damn!* It crosses $19,000. Someone raises to $19,500. I should let them get stuck with it there since I now feel they have just been egging me on. But I want it even so. $19,600. Mike knows it's my end and the mumble abruptly stops with a dramatic "Hah! Sold!"

We frame the Balance goal statement in the present tense since the subconscious only exists in the present tense.

Remodeling Begins

Karen is not saying how much she dislikes surprises and not knowing outcomes. Instead, she prepares extravagant breakfasts for the dogs — yogurt, vitamins, special oils for their coats, expensive kibble, chopped carrots and meats. Or she concentrates on helping her patients.

Margaret feels everything will work itself out but cannot communicate this, so she fixes what can be fixed around the house or the Chester property and concentrates on what we want to eat for supper — today's greens, yam soup, deviled eggs, fajitas or au gratin mac 'n cheese with green chile and sharp cheddar.

Thus begins our year of yelling badly. Our inferior functions emerge in periodic ague, as the fevers and emotional chills of remodeling unfold. If your house symbolizes your Body in your dreams, does the house that is your business symbolize the Body of your relationship? Probably.

And our relationship needs lots of loving care after I've willfully pushed us into a marriage of further financial responsibility. We neither talk of nor wish for real marriage, avoiding the debate of marriage equality laws, agreeing with Fran Lebowitz, who supports her gay friends but doubts their wish for inclusion in the two most repressive institutions — marriage and the military.

So I get on with it. I buy a new pair of goatskin construction gloves. I dig in a drainage tile from the front yard to the back to wick away excess water. I hire the first worker, a roofer, who is a neighbor. Relatively inexpensive and capable, but the type who doesn't clean up — which I didn't know about — that a job could be a job without cleaning up. So I grub through the grass for used nails and haul wheelbarrows of curled brittle shingles to the welcoming maw of the newly installed metal container at the back alley.

Karen and I don't seem to have anything new to say to each other during the weeks it takes to find someone to start the tear-out. Cory — medium build, nearly forty, from Shiloh, with a wife and young family — turns out to be our guy. It's cold winter now, although the soil isn't frozen under the little house, so he pries back the sloping floor of the front bedroom and digs in the quiet earth and basically builds a deck as the bedroom floor. This will be my main Balancing and treatment room. It will be cozy — new windows with a transom of stained glass, the north wall a warm orange hue to accompany the newly reupholstered Balance chairs and treatment table.

Next, Cory lugs his tools to the kitchen at the back of the long front room. With ripping, crashing, and prying, out go those tall white cupboards and the worn counters with chrome-handled drawers to some other purpose. He peels off pre-World-War-II-era linoleum and wallpaper from before the time when Chester returned from the war missing his upper bank of teeth.

Then he stalls. He's tired doing this alone or maybe he has another job lined up, perhaps in a heated building.

I am excited when Karen comes to see the progress.

"I can't really see that he's done anything except take out some cupboards," she says.

There's nowhere to sit except on the white-painted floorboards, so we stand in our winter coats in the long, wide main room. The brown metal gas heater that we used to call central heating and bring our clothes to dress in front of has been removed. There is only a built-in wooden hutch with glass door cabinets that the preacher who first lived here built.

"If we put in a wall here," I say, "between the pairs of double-hung windows, for the waiting room..."

"Then I'll be squeezed into a tiny adjusting room no bigger than the little room I have now," she says.

And I see now — now that we're actually talking it through — that Karen's room does look smaller than I thought it would.

"I can't live with this!" she explodes. "How can you think this could possibly work?"

I rush to take offense at this and respond with an oversensitive whinge.

"You are so juvenile and thoughtless," she continues. "And I so wish you could say what you mean in a reasonable period of time."

"But you are so critical and impossible to please."

"With good reason."

"And why do you always have to go into the red zone without warning?" I storm in return.

It does not go well. We forget how we actually appreciate and have, in relaxed moments, found our oppositeness to be humorous or helpful. Yet currently, we are in a state originally described by Gregory Bateson, the linguistic anthropologist and, for a time, husband of Margaret Mead, as "complementary schizmogenesis" — when two people's communicating styles continue to aggravate each other and escalate instead of resolving, and the only thing complementary about the communication is the schism that grows between participants.

As the blaze of our schizmogenesis begins to smoke itself out to a simple smolder, the room is again just cold and uncomfortable.

Then finally I come to. "OK so let's just take out the kitchen and its wall. Then we can enclose your room with a wall that puts the hutch in a hallway for supplements and supplies and another wall between you and the waiting room. You'll have a long room with two doors to the hallway, in front by the waiting room and in back across from the bathroom. Plus, you'll have the exit to the back porch."

"And I can put an oven out there for heating meals," she says. "That'll be good ... I told you we should take that wall out."

We imagine her future room with her library-table desk by the front wall, beautiful blinds on the newly oiled wooden windows, aquamarine-painted walls, adjusting table, barn-board cabinet for headrest paper and adjusting tools and a sofa for family members. Looks very pretty.

Then I add, "Cory says he's moving on to another job so we'll need someone new for the next part."

"Oh, sure. And who do you have lined up for that?"

As the heat rekindles, I feel we both wish we could try on the idea of a divorce. We could then cease hurling blame or murmuring satisfying retorts that do not accomplish moving to something calmer. Clearly, I have not yet discovered the secret to presenting a new step, whether project or problem. But how can I be confident and reassuring when I cannot possibly know?

"Can't you just see this as an unfolding project that's going to have changes that we need to adapt to?" I say.

"I think that you should have a better idea by now and should know where we're going."

"Now that you'll have that outside wall that was in the kitchen, you can put a window up there with stained glass and have beautiful western light."

"And open for air flow," she says.

Then, as always, Karen saves the day with her network of patients.

When a person comes to Balance for her relationship, it's impossible to tell if it's time for a divorce or a resolution, but it usually involves "accepting mySelf and the other person for who we truly are."

Remodeled

MARGARET: *I'm just discovering how I react to other people and their work ethic. I respond with feelings; you respond with critical thought.*

KAREN: *I agree. But you're the one who understands when they start talking about supporting walls, R-values and drywall texture. You imagine it.*

MARGARET: *I think I'm idealistically practical, just not always realistic. Actually assessing my attributes is difficult.*

KAREN: *Remember when you took the Meyers-Briggs Personality Test and answered the questions as how you'd like to be rather than how you are?*

Sherry Nilsson, Karen's patient for many years now, is a stained glass artist. She's going to craft vibrant glass flowers for front transom window accents and the piece for Karen's western sky window. I'm relieved when it turns out that her boyfriend, Guy, with a pony-tail of dark hair, a blue work shirt with the sleeves cut off and a pack of roll-your-own tobacco in the pocket and his friend, the drywall master, Ricky, can take up our cause. They will be ready for their next job in a few weeks. That will be mid-spring. They prefer working on old buildings rather than new construction.

It's closer to summer when they arrive. Immediately, they begin to tear off lathe and plaster, furring the upright studs for thicker, well-insulated walls. They figure out how to remove the kitchen wall and still support the load of the roof.

A sulky electrician, the husband of one of my Balance patients, has just put in new wire and circuit boxes—so we think. Yet, when Guy and Ricky are up in the attic they inform us that Sulky Bill has spliced together found wire with scrap circuit boxes. Luckily, they are competent and versatile and lay new wire and reconnect the switches and outlets. Then, surprisingly, Sulky Bill comes back to offer an apology for his poor workmanship—a requirement for the forgiveness step of his AA program. "I'm sorry. My wife and I were fighting at the time and I spited you two because of who you are and that you are her friends."

"Yes, well, I'm sorry too. I won't be paying you even so." I don't add that we know what it means to fight at home but we don't take it out on the rest of the world. I hope. Too much. In our work world, we generally like our patients but, even if we don't, we strive to help—not threaten their safety.

Karen and I are a united front against the know-it-all guys of the heating and cooling place who've done a sloppy job with ceiling vents for the expensive heat pump furnace, so they knock off some of the installation price.

Then Jimmie, the plumber, arrives. "What're ya doin?" he says, coming though the door in cutoffs and a T-shirt, tools strapped around his strong waist.

"Just looking to make a little progress," I say.

"That'll be no problem. I've come to install your gas wall heaters today and the sink and toilet tomorrow." He's pleasant and efficient — not fighting with his girlfriend.

Things between us get tense again before we have to return to Mindy's office at the bank for the money to finish. She's a refreshing new world, compared to old Turnipseed and Beanblossom, with light hair in a medium pageboy — no bangs. In a smart green jacket, with well-manicured nails, she readily takes us through the paperwork while her three children smile at us from pictures at the edge of her desk. This will make it about $60,000 when we're done. Karen and I bond again, while settling on light fixtures, the CD changer and speakers for each room.

Best of all is choosing the colored glass for the new windows. We arrive at Sherry's friend's house with tables and tables and boxes and boxes of colored glass. We're picking colors for two transom windows at the front of the house and the special 18-inch-square western sky window in Karen's room. Sherry's blonde hair is pulled back in concentration mode while her gray-blue eyes dance with artistic seduction as she woos us with color and cheer. We choose flaming-ember-colored orange lilies and intense purple pansies for my room, carmine-red petunias and heavenly blue morning glories for the waiting room, with emerald-green leaf accents for both. She giggles and serves us cups of coffee that go with the chocolate croissants we've brought from the City.

The tender truce of love and appreciation sustains as we decide on the glass colors for Karen's window. The center rose will be in shades of purply blackberry floating in a square of rippled prisms, surrounded by strips of royal blue between mid-point triangles and tiny corner squares of buttery gold. We laugh and celebrate Sherry's beautiful contributions.

From late summer through fall we're on a steady march to completion. Young Shiloh guys extract the old cement ramparts and regrade the yard. Karen's patients from Sigourney, Iowa City and Washington pour handsome sidewalks, lay carpet and install flooring. I observe that these are hardworking guys who appreciate low-force adjusting. In unity, the two of us oil and stain doors, windows and wood trim to honey perfection. Karen plants, waters and coaxes the new lawn while I paint the walls colors we've been meditating on for weeks.

Suddenly, we realize that we have just enough time to put together a grand opening for the first day of 2000 — the new millennium. Hasty plans are formulated and we push the last-minute details. Karen's very first Shiloh patient, Gary, hangs doors, trim and speakers and installs the glowing colors of the stained glass. With two days to go, I gather up all the painting drop cloths and have the metal refuse container loaded with the last remnants of these difficult months hauled away. We admire Karen's prospering lawn.

"Come inside," I say. I take her hand and lead her to the point between the door to my office and the near door to her office by the waiting room. "Stand right here. Now close your eyes, and..." I step over to the new stereo cupboard, switch on each room's speakers and push *Play*. The overture to *A Midsummer Night's Dream* dances and crescendos around us amid the new smells and colors of our accomplishment. "I love you. I love that we made it. That we made this."

It's fifty degrees and sunny on New Year's Eve day. Five or six athlete patients, girls and boys, relishing their fitness, make short work of moving our treatment tables and furniture in. The next morning, 1/1/2000, after the world did not end and computers did not fail, food arrives to fill a long table. The guest book accumulates ninety-nine names of people who've come to celebrate with us.

Mindy the Banker, wearing a raspberry-sherbet-colored jacket, meets my dad in the front room. He looks pretty smart — for a slightly stooped, gray-haired eighty-four year old. His Parkinson's meds are giving him a window to exude his out-in-the-world good humor and be truly present, albeit momentarily, for our success. The new hallway bustles with beaming faces of our oldest and youngest patients. Many friends from the surrounding towns fill plates with food and have party conversations. Others brag about what they did to contribute. Several Iowa City friends hang out on Karen's new sofa, laughing, talking, celebrating with us.

It's a bright moment for us in a widening community. We are now accessible to people who wouldn't think of becoming patients when we worked out of our home. We make the cover of *The Wellman Advance*. The *Cedar Rapids Gazette* shows interest. Many townspeople are here — a different group from the looky-loos that came to the auction. There's even an elderly couple who just believes in going to open houses and enjoying the food.

It's a day of accomplishment for both of us. The Body of our relationship has survived its near-death experience. Karen gloats, "We've got the nicest office space in town."

We design Balance goals to annihilate, then replace negative beliefs, so the goals we construct for the session initially test weak, before we've retuned the Body to embrace them.

Max and Me

MARGARET: *You know it's a good thing we played catch daily for that week before I had to go up and help the University Women's Center slow pitch team with their softball skills.*

KAREN: *I know. It was fun. How much help did they need?*

MARGARET: *Well, first we had to make sure their gloves fit. Then we fielded some simple grounders. Each infielder got an explanation on how to cover her base and back up other plays. Everyone hit a few pitched balls to get comfortable timing their swings, then hitting the ball and getting on base to score. Sometimes they forgot that scoring more points and winning was the goal. They strive to be egalitarian emancipators, you know.*

KAREN: *So, basically everything.*

MARGARET: *Sort of. We were easily at it for four hours. Glad I knew to treat my shoulder points and take a bunch of vitamin C and glucosamine sulfate, so I was no worse for the wear next day. Feel like playing now?*

It's a late-summer Saturday afternoon. The side and the main doors of Chester's old two-story garage are flung wide open. A radio on the workbench emits the singular musical thrum of a full baseball stadium and the famous play-by-play voices of Pat Hughes and Ron Santo calling a Cubs game. I am disassembling some wooden junk to build a cute upright bench for the front porch of our new clinic. Now and then I pause and listen to imagine a play, a slide, dust in the mouth or hope from a crack of the bat.

Then an aged, banged-up white pickup pulls up in the back alley. The current old-man mayor, Max Moffatt, flings open the driver's door to an accompanying metallic *crack*. He huffs himself out, cane first, limping and murmuring along in striped overalls as he heads for my open garage door. He's a loud, retired nobody who likes to meddle and micromanage the city workers and various town boards, yet take no definitive town business action. Karen, who sits on the library board, says he is always calling the state bureaucrats with petty gripes and inane questions.

I turn down the volume of the ballgame. "Hello, Max," I say loudly so he can hear. "How're you doin' this beautiful afternoon? Come in. Have a seat." I gesture to my prize garage chair, a sturdy wood-framed hulk with garish plaid cushions.

As he pitches himself into the seat, I remember someone telling me that he broke his foot when his truck rolled over it. I do not inquire.

"Just fine. Just fine," he booms as he settles into the worn cushion, his white socks revealing themselves above his work shoes. I wonder how he can be just fine with that foot. We do not know each other so I do not inquire about the wife who is likely responsible for his clean socks and who also recklessly allows him out on the street to wreak havoc on town business. He makes himself comfortable and seems content to take his time getting to the point. "Well, the council has recommended the town officially create a park board," he says, looking around at the rugged handiwork of the building. "I heard you might be interested."

He stops again. And I guess he thinks that was a question. He's come blustering by to recruit me as a volunteer, always preferring to be out and about rather than making a simple phone call.

"Yes, I am interested," I say. "I think parks are important. And we have really good ones, what with North Park's pavilion and ball diamonds, South Park's versatility by the creek, having the summer rodeo or the bikers' camp, and the little postage stamp of a park downtown."

He himself has no interest in talking about them or considering plans. Just on a mission to be busy. "The appointments will officially be made at next week's town council meeting," he says. Then, not a guy to expand his conversation to greater subjects, after delivering the message, he heaves himself upright again and totters back to his pickup. As I turn back to my bench, I hear the crack and slam of him getting on his way.

The ballgame is over now, so I ponder these new circumstances. For the longest time I have kept out of committees and public participation. This might be a nice way to break that pattern. I can't help review the bits and pieces of my public participation in the past.

There were a few high-school triumphs in speech, art and sports. Among the best was an invitation to an All-State Girl Scout Encampment in California. But it

curdled into my greatest disappointment when someone decided the patrol leaders' inspirational final-day
event should be an all-camp church service and I was
left reading a lumpy Bible verse. I thought we girls
should not just passively worship, but inspire ourselves
to "do our duty to God and our country and help other
people at all times," as our motto proclaimed.

This was followed by the involutions of coming out,
the unveiling of women's liberation and my mother's
choice to take a careful measure of her many pills and
skip out. I hardly knew myself in private, let alone in
the public. It was more fun to paint my fingernails red
and play softball in short shorts in the summer heat.
This did require stepping it up on the field, pitching,
sliding and making double plays from second base
with razor-edged cleats coming for my exposed flesh.

After that, I learned whom to believe, how to trust
myself in an assortment of jobs, and I completed my degrees. But there was still no time for the public except as
a brooding background strategist to help a friend out of a
predicament or writing workplace newsletters as respite
from monotony, still quite far from the foreground.

To be sure, in the past few years I've ventured to
give a few community presentations, as the public
wants "alternative medicine" viewpoints, and I do my
best to explain the inscrutable aspects of Balancing.
But we are now part of this community. So. OK. I commit. Parks are important. It will be good to participate
in something meaningful.

On the night of the first meeting I arrive at Town

Hall and slide into a seat at the corner of the long wood-en council table. There are six of us — two men, four women. There's gloomy-faced Doris Yoder who lives down our street and spends so much time bent over quilts, stitching, that she can barely turn her head. The new Methodist preacher is a soft-spoken, gray-haired, thoughtful-looking guy. A thirty-something energetic woman is dressed in sporty workout clothes. And then there's cheerful, ubiquitous Murvel Walker, a retired schoolteacher who's come back to her family home in Wellman to spend her time volunteering.

The other man is Marvin Stutzman, dark-haired, nice-looking, likeable, fifty years old and yet unwill-ing to assert his own mind, if he knows it. His wife, Laverne, that is Verny, is the tough one. She's a super-visor at the plastics factory in Kalona and has been a regular patient of Karen's. Earlier in the summer Mar-vin called us on a Saturday afternoon saying that Verny was dizzy and disoriented. We went to their house to see what was happening and found her staggering about saying incoherent things, with a weird odor about her. Marvin pointed to the camper. Opening the door released a bomb of Clorox bleach fumes. Verny had been cleaning the refrigerator with full strength bleach and no ventilation. Back in the house we told her that she had overdosed herself with chlorine and needed to deeply breath fresh air, take 5,000 mg of vita-min C and perhaps call Poison Control to see if they had any suggestions. Poison Control was no help and the emergency folks couldn't miss a chance to make a little money. When we called the next day to see how she was doing we learned that they had to freak out and go to the emergency room and spend the rest of the evening getting a CAT scan. Naturally, they were happy to report it was negative. He's simple, but OK to deal with.

I am looking to set a meeting date that will work for everyone, except that Mayor Max, still a harrumphing presence, horns right in. "I think you should elect officers now," he says, bullying us into rapid action.

"Perhaps if we wait till our first scheduled meeting we'll have a better idea…" I begin.

The others are quiet so he blows right on saying, "Nominations for president are open. Second place will be vice-president."

Blindsided. So I do the most appropriate thing and nominate Marvin. Marvin nominates me. Mayor Max calls for the vote. The gavel whaps my plans to fragments. I am the new president of the Park Board.

I discover I am not so fluent in positive words, so it takes a surprisingly long time to formulate the positive version of the belief that needs to be changed.

George

KAREN: *Is this too much — being on the Park Board?*

MARGARET: *I like getting good at running a meeting and we seem to be getting a lot done. I told you about my memory from second grade, with my tall imposing teacher who made me nervous. She asked us what we thought living into the next millennium might be like. And I told her I was here for the Renaissance ... remember?*

KAREN: *Yes. Pretty surprising.*

MARGARET: *I know, to me too when I remembered. Maybe this is working toward it, although I thought we'd be getting closer by now in the larger world. Surely it's begun in quiet quarters around the earth. Either that or it doesn't start until there's complete destruction.*

A demolition derby? What the ...?" I stop myself from saying this out loud. *Just listen. Just listen.*

Here's George Stegner at a spring Park Board meeting. His long-sleeved plaid/flannel shirt smooths over his ballooning belly as his suspenders stretch to hold his khaki pants and their straining zipper. "The Lion's Club wants to host its fundraising demolition derby in the South Park like we have in the past," he says in a voice that carries throughout the room.

I recall that over the years this grassy plot along Smith Creek at the south border of town, with its sturdy wooden stand for announcers and judges, gets used as a summer weekend campground for bikers who motorcycle in, set up camp and then head up to the Chat for supper and beer; once for a traveling one-tent circus with tiny trick dogs, a pony and a precious little elephant; and the occasional itinerant preacher who comes to spread the supremacy of fear. It's also been torn up regularly for mini-rodeos and previous demo derbies.

I wince at the request, although the rest of the board seems placid enough, as he continues, "We move those big felled tree trunks down there to enclose the arena. We'll use the bleachers but also let people back their pickups to the edges and sit in the truck beds on lawn chairs. We water the grass so it's soaked, muddy and hard to get traction. Lots of cars register from nearby towns. It's our biggest fundraiser."

He slides a flyer mock-up across the table. It has pictures of cars before and after: sedans with roll bars, pounded-out fenders, doors tied shut, glass windows removed. The exhaust pipes are rerouted like little chimneys straight off the engine up through the hoods. Cars are spray painted with numbers and sponsor logos at various levels of artistic elegance. "After" pictures show buckled doors, dragging bumpers, curled and smashed fenders. Mud is splashed and spattered across the cars and the grinning, whiplashed drivers. There is an added line at the bottom that reads "No Impeariels." Bold type but misspelled. Apparently the old Chrysler Imperial was so well made that it would destroy any car it ran into.

As George talks he rests his left hand on the table and I notice that his fingers do not fully extend. His middle finger lays on his palm and the hand tries to function around it. It's been that way for so long he seems to think nothing of it.

We vote. It's a go for a Saturday in August. "Good job, George." I reach out to shake his hand. He accepts my right hand in his, grasping both our hands with his left pokey-fingered one.

Later that spring, I too become a member of the Lion's Club. I plan to cram earplugs in my ear canals and go watch the boys tear up the terrain in their carefully refashioned machines. Perhaps, I'll catch the Beachy Amish women sweating in their bonnets and colored dresses, their young families sunburned and squealing from the beds of their pickups. It's a way to observe what I call "metal sports" and participate in community events, but avoid the pretentiousness of our Rotary, run mostly by our banker and his cronies.

So, along with ninety-year-old Milton Rediger, Orville's brother, and the couple who owned the downtown café years ago, here's George again. Now in a short-sleeved, yellow-plaid shirt and plain-framed glasses, his dark hair in a bit of a comb-over on his smooth, sunbaked head.

He lives three blocks north of our house, on upper Main Street. His wife, June, was Karen's patient the first year we opened, helped make her reputation, come to think of it, in a different sort of way from the miracle-cure kind of way. She was a kind, gregarious woman with considerable back pain and a suspect history—a previous cervical cancer diagnosis, surgery to remove her uterus and an ovary, subsequent night sweats and prescribed estrogen. Some years later, the back pain began. She was diagnosed with simple osteoarthritis from a CT scan so she came for chiropractic care. Karen saw her three or four times but recognized the results were not what they should be, suggesting she return for further medical diagnosis. MRI showed cancer had metastasized to her lumbar spine. She told her many friends that it was Karen who got her to the proper diagnosis. She died the following year. Since then, George has lived alone.

When Murphy and I walk up our street at night, I peer at George's white-sided two-story house with a front porch crammed full of furniture, tools and an old stove. I've never had reason to go inside but I imagine it full of more piles and the odors of a bachelor's kitchen. Dinty Moore stew cans, fresh asparagus wilting on a stained aqua formica countertop.

He has a garden at his little farm acreage north of town on the road to Frytown. Maybe it's twenty acres — for hay and a little crop, a small barn for the two horses that he seldom has time to work and ride with his day job teaching at the high school and his night job planting and harvesting those acres. The place is surrounded by land vultures who would swallow up his property in a minute, tear down his barn, the out buildings and corral, then plow it to smithereens.

I hear he's Republican, along with those Rotary guys, even if he doesn't dress preppy. He drops by our office one afternoon to bring by Lion's Club stuff and sits in the rocking chair by the window and massages his injured hand. It gives me an opening to ask what happened. "A bullet," he says, massaging under the rogue finger. "I was bent forward with my hands behind my back. The bullet missed my body but went right through my palm."

I don't ask about further circumstances, just go over to look more closely and ask him why they didn't remove the errant finger. He holds it out to show me and I take the warm back of his hand in my palm. "You might have greater use of your forearm muscles to strengthen your grip and not just be using these finer palm muscles if this middle finger wasn't in the way," I say. I touch the spastic finger with my other hand. His hands are warmer than my own. "Could you have this looked into?"

"The VA did what they did," he says.

I suggest my hand-surgeon friend could examine it for him. But I see that he will just proudly endure as he has all along, like he shouldn't expect what I think might be an improved medical outcome. It occurs to me that his Republican presidential candidate would think him a good soldier. This is the hand of a hard-working, involved guy, yet he's got no grasp of how to improve his grip.

I relinquish his hand and step back. "Do you think your namesake George Bush's ideas will be helpful to you? Like more tax cuts for rich people?"

He rouses himself from the rocking chair with a swell of pleasure. His suspenders stretch as his shoulders straighten. I get the idea he wants to prolong an extravagant feeling. "Well, you never know when you're going to be able to take advantage of such an opportunity yourself," he says. The casual, almost-scripted reply hangs in the air as he prepares to leave the waiting room. He suppresses a grin, working his mouth like the words are just delicious and he's shared a naughty joke. For just a moment his veneer of fearful worry has lifted. "I've got to be going," he says, not wanting to break the spell of his imagined riches and braggadocio with mundane Lion's Club business.

"Thanks for the papers, George." I leave the door open for just a bit to air out the disquieting idiocy of his words. More demolition to come I imagine. Only this time, "Impeariels" take on the middle class.

Retuning the Body to embrace new beliefs may involve clearing meridians that are stuck in negative patterns that support old, unwanted beliefs.

Political Abdication

Packing up after a weekend of camping with the corgis at Lake Darling.

KAREN: *Can you bring the utensils from the fire pit? Oh, and take down the clothesline? I've got the towels.*

MARGARET: *No problem; it's just a clove hitch.*

KAREN: *Is that some fancy Girl Scout thing?*

MARGARET: *Sort of — one of my favorite knots anyway. A firm knot when it's holding weight, but otherwise just rope wrapped twice around a tree and through itself; comes undone quite easily.*

By mid-2001, we've ended the dissimulations of the Clinton years, having lost any measure of diversity in telecommunications ownership, given a wink and a nod to the big banks to regulate themselves and continued incarcerating a disproportionate number of the disempowered. Thankfully, the full fever of impeachment threats and musings about the blue dress are behind us and most ramifications of acquiescing the middle ground will come later. Now, we have the twangy, buddy-buddy, frat-boy talk of George Bush the younger, with his sneering vice-president and possibly malevolent cabinet. Politics is a wearying subject.

I'm taking great satisfaction in Mary Daly's feminist *Wickedary* from the late eighties. Her super-smart, wicked, Xena-like attitude prevails as she "perches on the fence of the fatherland and observes its fatuous 'reality.'" She has taught me the delicious word "snool," with its seductive sound. To snool is to dominate, bully or reduce to submission. The snool is the cringing abject recipient of the bullying; certainly not a word from the Constitution with its "protect," "defend," "uphold" and "common good" sorts of words.

Here in Wellman, the town limps along in faded glory, yet glows benevolently on the surface. The blond-brick Municipal Building roosts at the corner of Main and Fourth Streets, just a block east of our new office. It's nicely appointed for a tiny town. The council room is paneled like a courtroom and there is a full-sized basement for meetings, from AA to family gatherings or political caucusing. There's plenty of room for the town clerk and her part-time staff to run the business of the town and our natural gas coop. Patricia Kemp, the clerk and keeper of the town's delicate secrets, is an astute-eyed oldest daughter who affects a mild, yet judicious, manner. She is conveniently married to the son of a former mayor.

Her ex-mayor father-in-law, Ward, is short, stout, bespectacled and garrulous, formerly the town's farm implement dealer. Once, on the sidewalk outside the Municipal Building, he's eager to tell me a story. "In the early seventies a traveler comes to town," he says, while hitching his pants around his rotund belly. "He seems like an enterprising guy and offers to paint the town's flagpole." Mayor Ward scratches his balding head. "And I agree to his $100 bid." As he relives the memory, he stands back, gesturing up at the twenty-foot pole in its little patch of grass by the entryway. "So, I watch the guy lay a drop cloth around the base of the flagpole, then immerse a large rag in a bucket of shiny silver paint, then gather it in his arms." Ward looks at me like he still doesn't believe this event. "He shinnies up the pole with the rag, wraps it round the pole and slides back down." Mayor Ward's mouth is open, his tongue massaging his lower lip in remembering his joyful amazement. Then he turns and grins his appreciation. "That pole got painted in all of ten minutes. I paid him his check on the spot."

Here's a glimpse into a small town crack in time. And so, too, Karen and I each have chances to participate in town life. Karen serves a couple of years on the town library board. As a voracious, lifelong reader, she is book savvy and has helped recruit a new librarian — one of her patients, of course, a woman who is kind, experienced and will not censor the Harry Potter books because they are too "magical."

For my part, it's been a profitable year at the Park Board. Everyone has assignments. Monthly meetings are efficient. We each report on our projects. Celia Strangeheart, in her magenta jumpsuit, reports, "We have new barrel flower containers throughout downtown at Freeman's Grocery, the Historical Society, Semler's Hardware, the Frame Shop, Pretty Styles Hair Salon and Starbeck Photography. The owners are getting used to watering each morning so the flowers are doing well." She giggles and says, "They look so pretty."

Doris Yoder, quilter extraordinaire, oversees a potluck, game day and a family concert at North Park. Vice President Marvin Stutzman coordinates with the Lions Club about the demolition derby in South Park. The new Methodist preacher brings a list of plantings that will thrive under the giant walnut tree at City Hall including arbor vitae, hostas, lilies and phlox. Townspeople will donate bulbs or cuttings from their gardens. We vote to apply no more herbicide or pesticide at the town parks. Wellman gets honored as a Tree City. There have been several planting days with grade school and high school students. We teach how to successfully plant trees and discuss the importance of urban forestry. Trees reduce crime, cool neighborhoods and provide a minor counterbalance to those trees continually bulldozed on farm acres so the eighteen-row planters and harvesters can travel the miles-long fields and not have to turn around.

One morning I'm behind the counter in the sunny office of the town clerk, getting the Trees Forever files, when Mayor Max limps in, barking loudly out of the vacuum of his gray matter. I see cool Patricia's jaw set in an uncharacteristic manner and I realize she has reached a level of frustration well beyond personal distaste. He has been causing serious problems, greater than being loud and obnoxious, creating a self-centered turmoil wherever he is.

I sometimes wonder how a wife can let such a husband leave the house to inflict inept and expensive pain on the town. Perhaps she's glad to see his back.

He aggravates the town workers who fix the streets, water mains and gas lines with his micromanagement. He barges in on Karen's library board meetings and undermines them by calling the state library administration to inquire about time-wasting trivialities. Now, three consecutive sewage facility managers have quit in the middle of constructing our new waste disposal plant because he stands over them with peevish incessancy. As the months have passed, the town is being fined $1,000 a day for our seeping sewage system down near Smith Creek. I think he makes the perfect gregarious greeter for meetings and functions like the farmer's market. But as a leader he refuses to make decisions and delays actions even if the council is in agreement. Town business has turned to sludge.

I find this perturbing and don't want to be among the cringers to his bully-bungling snoolishness. Giving him any advice or critique is laughable. Besides, he got elected so he wins. I come to feel I must at least put this out to the public, since he's affecting the town's reputation and pocketbook. After struggling with this through the fall and into the new year, I decide to take an action. After all, since I am in a volunteer position, I can publicly resign in protest. Perhaps the council can stop submitting to the belligerence. I notify my board members and the council.

It's a cold January night under the fluorescent hues of the council chamber. The meeting is packed. A few winter jackets emit scents of fried dinner from the café. The council members, four men and a woman, sit at the elongated table up front, not conversing with Mayor Max. He sits, florid-faced, his arms crossed in the center seat. I am two-thirds of the way back sitting on my wool coat, having an add-on slot before the main agenda. My turn comes after several citizen comments and the gray, nondescript, I-am-the-victim-looking guy who is publicly announcing himself as a sex offender, intending to live with his sister just down the street.

I take my time as attention turns to me. As I stand and look around a bit, the previous speaker's words dissipate in the crowded room. There's a bit of postural rearrangement. Then, it's time — deep breath, smile. "Thank you, everyone. It's been a great year for our new Park Board." More shifting in the seats. "Our members did a wonderful job with park activities, from new playground equipment to becoming a Tree City. And I have been honored to serve you." Past tense. It's begun.

I pause again. I feel like the truth-teller in the dysfunctional family, bringing up the obvious problem that no one wants to confront but everyone has been tripping over. It's not something that actually happens in my biological family, but tonight I feel … a what? Connection? More like a duty.

"Tonight I am resigning as your Park Board president. I feel it's my mission to publicly call attention to a problem that we've all been dealing with. The problem is with our mayor's style of micromanagement. It is creating poor morale for the town workers. It has caused us to lose three managers at the sewage facility.

We have been paying $1,000 a day for our faulty system and the repair keeps getting delayed due to our mayor's method of meddling and micromanaging." There is now an undercurrent of agreement going through the crowd. Several part-time contractors are nodding. The council members are noticeably listening, even if they are not commenting. They do not look to the mayor for their opinions. They aren't really looking at me.

In for a penny, in for a pound. Or, more appropriately, time to go whole hog.

I continue as the mayor remains unmoved in his crossed-arms posture, "We have people who would volunteer for committees, boards or other functions who just don't want to participate." More heads nod and there is an assenting murmur of agreement. No signs of objection from Mayor Max. "The problem for us is to not get sidetracked into irrelevant conversations and inertia, when action is needed. As members of the council, you have the ability to get business moving, to make decisions, to follow through even if the mayor can't commit. And I encourage you to do so. Thank you."

The council members, in a moment of true relief, laugh and clap in full agreement. They radiate a moment of clarity, share the embrace of solidarity and lucid possibility. There are echoes of support. Others chime in with their approval.

And then, it's done.

Mr. Mayor just sits there unaffected. No one responds to me; they are buoyant with each other. Because of the surprising outburst of their response, I feel gratified. Perhaps it's a staying influence. Task completed; there's nothing for me to do but leave and let them get on with the business part of the meeting.

In the cold light of the following morning, once more at the clerk's office to wrap up some business, one of the council members comes in. I smile. He nods. Sort of. There's no conversation, no follow up. It becomes a moment of nervous embarrassment as though that moment of complete unanimity didn't even happen. It's more like we saw each other naked and today are embarrassed instead of intimately pleased. He leaves as fast as he came.

For the tiniest increment of time I wonder if abdication was the correct move. Then, I remember that this was my unique opportunity to speak sincerely, to protect, defend and uphold — to stand up to the snool. I took it and the rest is about them and their willingness to responsibly tend the town.

Now I've become the head of the Tree Committee. Trees may be inscrutable, but they stand tall and provide shade, oxygen, stature and beauty — not such political weariness.

I think of Brain Gyms,® the hand/eye movements, along the path of an infinity symbol, as rearranging brain circuitry, creating space for new ideas.

The Passage That Opens the Door

KAREN: *You know we could have set up our practice and been in New Mexico all this time if you hadn't felt the need to stick around for your father.*

MARGARET: *I know. It's because I had such a good relationship with him before the age of eleven. I was foolish and optimistic that there could be something now.*

KAREN: *He fell into that old-man arrogance, having a new wife to dote on him.*

MARGARET: *Instead of getting therapy and understanding his first wife's suicide, he was in a rush to remarry — so he'd have someone to wash his socks.*

On a Monday morning in March of 2003, I get an eight o'clock call from my sister Barb. She's five years younger and had a poor time at home during her high school years, as our parents grew apart. She has made a good life for herself and her daughter as an office manager for a law firm. Our dad, eighty-seven-year-old Robert Louis Hansen, has finally passed. Barb fills me in that Second Wife and her "real" daughter, from her first marriage, have already been to the funeral home to make all the arrangements.

Accommodating his death has been out of my hands since a year and a half ago — since the fall evening that Dad's second thirty-year wife called to say I better come because he was in the hospital. I found him in a private room, wearing a gown with blue piping, resting quietly in his tilted-up bed. He was conscious, but fading. When he saw me, he gathered his wits and smiled with feeble ardor. He had a plan. "Peg (That's what the family calls me.) is going to go round and get the Cadillac. (We didn't have one.) Peg is going to drive me home," he said in his worn-out but lilting voice.

I said, "I'll be happy to, Dad."

Second Wife whimpered from the other side of the room, "But, Bob, you have a home." He looked confused at that. That night I wrote our last conversation down in my notebook.

I returned the next day to send him on his way and discovered all kinds of snake-like electrodes hooked up to his head. "Just some tests," the staff said when I demanded they stop and take them out so he could be comfortable. By then, they had mostly revived him and determined what brought him in — a bilateral thalamic stroke. The stroke had accomplished what decades of drinking and pretended happiness aspired to do — wipe out his emotional pain and memory. Second Wife was pleased with the superficial recovery. For her it was much better than a healthy and timely death.

He recovered enough to go a well-appointed nursing home. I didn't think it was the home he wanted me to drive him to. His life existed between bed and wheelchair. A "memory book" hung like a kid's backpack behind his chair so he could supposedly relearn who his family was. For certain, it contained neither our mother nor Karen.

I visited a few times. The place was nice, and why not for a guy with too-good insurance? Second Wife was always there, hovering in devotion to his dependency. As I approached, along the well-kept tiled hallway to the atrium, she would say loudly and knowingly, "Well, Bob, guess who's here to visit?" I'd see him smile abstractedly, unaware that he should grab the memory book and make sense of it. "Why, it's Peg, isn't it?"

I gave in to the process. We'd already had our last conversation and the benevolent celebration at the opening of our office. At my final visit, he had no body qi, no physical resilience. He was unconscious, trembling on his side, bereft of his former greatest generation ease. So much harder to let go this way. I just whispered in his ear to say, "I love you. It's OK to go, with or without the Cadillac."

To prepare for the funeral, now that he's finally relieved of his earthly body, I buy a new Garfield & Marks suit and Karen gets out beautiful turquoise earrings and bracelet to wear with black pants and an Eileen Fisher gauzy top. At the visitation, I see few family friends, most having passed before him. One neighbor from the old neighborhood, and Mom's and Second Wife's bridge group, is deeply kind and seems to understand the whole dynamic. I wish I had known to keep in touch throughout the decades.

One of the pallbearers was my high school steady boyfriend—for two and a half years. He was a poet and "furthest-back-bench" of the football team sort of guy, who married a girl from my college dorm floor. I saw him a few times in college, still unable to exactly explain why I stopped going to my locker by way of his locker midway through our senior year. I have learned from the movie *Romy and Michele's High School Reunion* that he was probably at the fringe of the A group, or definitely a high B. I knew he had become a lawyer (but, didn't he hate that?) for the Rock Island Arsenal where my dad worked for thirty years. I remember now our promise that if we weren't married by age seventy we would rethink things.

I hug his expanded girth. He returns a broad-faced smile. "Dennis, I'd like you to meet my partner for nearly twenty years now. Karen Zakar."

His eyes fall closed, his body briefly clenches forward, hands crossing his middle, then with an abrupt conversational pirouette he puts out a well-manicured hand and says, "It's a pleasure to meet you."

I am shocked for him. Does he wonder why my parents barbecued and played golf with him and Victoria, never saying anything real about me? I still feel bad about our senior year, when I was sixteen and knew nothing except that, although he was funny and I liked him, fervent kissing was becoming nauseating — not something I was comfortable confessing to him. I hadn't yet integrated gayness.

Although part of me wants to drink margaritas, share a bong and tell all these things, I realize that we're the unwanted, mandatory guests at our own family's Midwestern, Presbyterian gathering. So we sit and make nice over pale potato salad and cheese cubes until Dennis excuses himself to go pick up Victoria, who couldn't come. Barb and Karen and I continue to talk about Second Wife's perpetual disapproval of us, but that she did care for Dad.

We remember good things about Dad, though Karen has no experiences to add. Barb remembers a story from when she was twelve, when she and Dad called me at Camp Conestoga where I was a Girl Scout counselor. I was dishing up supper for my table of campers in the dining hall when I was called to the telephone. Barb told me that they hit a record number of badminton returns! 423! They called again the next night to say they had broken last night's record. 424!

Then Barb recalls her last "conversation" with her father. She was making her way from Chicago along the frosty Mississippi River Road, three mornings ago. In the tree-lined valley and delicate pale light, she noticed an eagle flying at her speed just above the wide, steamy, late-winter river. The eagle rose over the trees above Barb's car, then flew along in front of her. It was beautiful and honoring. Then, the eagle soared out of sight above the river. The clock in her car said 7:22 a.m. That's how she knew when her father died. We all cry at that.

To have a little more time to herself before going on to the house, Barb stopped in the little river town of Buffalo for breakfast. When she arrived at the house, Second Wife fussed about, telling her what she must be feeling since she missed seeing her Dad. Barb said it was OK because she knew when he died.

"You can't have known that," Second Wife said.

Barb said with certainty, "I know when it was. It was 7:22."

Second Wife wasn't pleased for her. Instead, she smarted, acting her true nature. She was piqued that Barb knew a thing that she alone was supposed to know. That Barb had somehow won a competition existing between us all through the years and, she was not telling how. We all laugh at that.

When the conversation finally fades to quiet, Karen says, "Well, at least when we do retire to New Mexico there will be nothing holding us here. The door has opened."

The book As You Believe, *by Barbara Dewey, explains the quantum physics of how the universe constantly blinks on and off, allowing change to occur in an instant.*

Dina's Story

KAREN: *I have a fairly new patient named Leland Smith. He and his wife, Connie, have four kids and live at the top of our street. They used to be in an intentional community in Illinois. They came here when the community fell apart due to the leader being a sexual predator. Now, they and their friends from that same community, Ken and Fay Landing and their three children, all go to the most liberal of the Mennonite churches out north of town.*

MARGARET: *How did you get along?*

KAREN: *Just fine. He likes to talk about teaching Love and prayer to his students at the Iowa Mennonite School. He teaches the senior devotions class plus mathematics to keep grounded. The only hitch is Connie came by later. I got the idea she thinks I'm trying to seduce him.*

MARGARET: *Poor thing. What did you tell her?*

KAREN: *I reassured her and we connected OK. She's actually the butch one of the pair.*

K aren comes into my treatment room. "Can you hear me when you're upside down?" she asks.

I'm in a yoga head-and-shoulder stand against the wall. My drooping trouser legs reveal blue socks in gray Mephistos. I give a red-faced smile and an "Mmmh Hmmh."

"Well I just saw Kay's mother. What an obstinate, difficult person. Poor Kay and Jeff having to live next to them. Anyway, she needs her muscles checked. Her right knee pain doesn't go away with adjusting."

"Mmmh Hmmh. Hwwolldishe?"

"Do you think I can understand you?"

I relent to join the conversation. Bend knees, tuck gently, flop right side up. Coming to stand while smoothing my cuffs, I say, "Sure. No problem. How old is she?"

"Late sixties. She's pretty energetic, except for the knee…and difficult. Kay getting her mother to come to us is something of a miracle."

Kay and Jeff are well-known potters from Frogtown. Frogtown is a tiny town about an hour west of here on our little Highway 22, also known for its occasional acres-big flea markets. Not long after we opened, around twelve years ago, Kay walked into Karen's adjusting room as a new patient. "My lamp!" she exclaimed about the one piece of art we could afford — a soft-shouldered ceramic beauty with a landscape of blues on dappled pinks.

On the appointed day, Dina Bollinger limps back in. The process is new for her so she's alternately fascinated and irascible. She tugs at the jacket of the light-blue tracksuit covering her roundy but sturdy body as I explain about testing muscles and finding related points that will strengthen them. "Why didn't my medical doctor tell me about this?"

A slew of untamed thoughts ensue before I calmly say, "Well, these are concepts that originated in the chiropractic field." Most people seem to follow right along even when the concept is new, allowing the discovery to inform them. Dina is more reluctant and unsure since this is something her medical doctor doesn't know, so she may be uncertain whether or not she can believe it.

In spite of her caution and touchy nature, I feel as though we have the beginning of a new and positive connection. I am cautiously optimistic that she understands her homework. She has her visual aid. On a white paper with the outline of a woman's body I've drawn x's to mark the points she needs to treat on her belly, the top edge of her pubic bone and along her thighs to activate muscles of her thigh, hip and lower leg.

I walk her out to meet her patiently waiting husband. "We'll see you in a week, Dina, to see how you are improving." She hears but doesn't look back.

We head to the house for some lunch — steamed spinach with hardboiled egg dashed with a little left-over onion dip. Others may be made afraid of fat and egg yolks, but my satiety monitors are not persuaded. As I start back down to the office, I am stopped in the entryway beside our original adjusting table that now sits next to the bannister. It is the sturdy blue vinyl one that our angels Ginny and Peter helped us buy. Although we planned to find it a new home, we got it this far and then it became useful one summer day. One of the tree trimmers, hacking our ash tree in half to make room for the telephone lines, overreached with his extended chainsaw from his elevated basket and felt his mid-back seize up. Since he was right outside our home practice, his friend marched him to the door. He was in his grimy work clothes with no time to clean up, so Karen gave him a couple precise thumps there on that table and sent him back to the job. Afterward, it became a fixture here for just such occasions.

Today, though, I discover a folded newspaper surreptitiously placed on it, apparently while we were in the kitchen. I pick it up to see that it's a national Mennonite Church publication. The top center article is about the importance of being open and welcoming to gay people in one's congregation. There's no note attached. I carry it into the kitchen where Karen's finishing lunch. "Hey honey, look what someone left for us." She looks up from her nearly empty plate and Kinsey Milhone mystery. "Who do you supposed left this?"

She takes the paper, glances at the front page and then drops it on the table. "Someone who wants us to know they are struggling with our cause...maybe Leland and Connie's friends Fay and Ken Landing. They are always earnest and sincere about inclusiveness. Maybe they want to counterbalance conversations going on in the conservative churches."

"Well, that is a thoughtful offering. I don't suppose they can help but confront the subject now that AIDS and ACT UP have put it front and center. It's weird to just be going along with our workweek and then be distracted by someone else's problem that they have made about us."

The week goes by and Dina returns for her second appointment. There's still some pain, but she shows signs of improvement. Remarkably she has made an effort to do her homework and most of the muscles are strengthening. And yet, we discover an important muscle that has not strengthened — that long Sartorius that runs from the side of the hip, across the thigh to the inside of the knee. When weak it slackens the connection between hip and knee just enough to allow the joint to be slightly out of alignment and cause pain. Our next step will be to give her nutritional support for her adrenal glands since adrenal glands relate to the Sartorius in the organ / muscle relationship. If the adrenals are overtaxed, the muscle is often affected. I have her place a popular supplement capsule under her tongue, then recheck the muscle and she sees that it holds strong. She agrees to take this capsule in the morning with her breakfast, and perhaps one with lunch if she has a stressful day. She seems to feel more optimistic. I reschedule her for one more check-in next week and send her on her way.

The following week, Kay calls to cancel Dina's appointment for the next day. "Dr. Silva says that the licorice in the supplement will raise her blood pressure. She told Mom that it was dangerous for her to take it."

I feel my regularly low blood pressure take an uninvited surge. "Well, tell your mother that her supplement has deglycyrrhizinated licorice, designed to not affect her blood pressure. And her body tested strong for it." I calm my voice while I shake the phone in midair. "I'll erase her from the schedule."

"I'm sorry, Margaret. My mother's attracted to conflict."

"I understand. We were crossing into uncharted waters for her, even though I was ever hopeful. But really Ines Silva has no business doing such a thing. And, of course, it's your mother. Don't worry, Kay. Thanks for the call." I recount the story to Karen.

"That certainly pushes my M.D. button," she says.

"I know. I'm going to call her." I pause, thinking aloud. "Didn't we think it would be good to have her in this area with her background in herbal and traditional medicines? That she would be a great person to refer to?"

Dr. Ines has come to Shiloh from a sister church in Brazil. She works in Sigourney, twenty miles down the road in a family practice clinic. It is owned by the University of Iowa Hospitals and Clinics, whose encroaching tentacles have spread beyond their formerly restrained and acclaimed tertiary health care role into primary care across the state.

My heart is pounding as I open the English Valley phone book. Would I do that to Silva? Take someone off a medication, even if the person tests weak for it? That happens often enough. I think of the patients we have who have failed in the medical system, like the woman with her three-foot stack of Mayo charts — a compendium of what diagnoses she doesn't have, who still has the same pain she started with, and all those who chose surgery first but are no better or are perhaps worse. OK, no mentioning what it looks like from our end.

The phone is ringing. "Yes, Dr. Silva, this is Dr. Margaret Hansen from Wellman." There's a bright response on the other end. "We share a patient—Dina Bollinger from Frogtown. Do you recall you took her off her adrenal support supplement?"

Now she remembers and starts into the high blood pressure excuse with a rising Portuguese accent. "Yes, I was told that was the reason. Did you think to call me to find out about the supplement, that it was formulated with deglycyrrhizinated licorice? You must not have seen the bottle or you would know." I can't believe I'm giving her a way out. "Do you also recall that she is a difficult patient? That it's a challenge to create a good rapport with her? Why would you do that and not call me with your concerns?"

She bluffs a little, has no apology, but knows that she's cost me any relationship with my patient. I let her off easily, having made the point. "Thank you for taking my call."

I know why and how this came about. I know the longstanding AMA versus Chiropractic rancor. I know that we see those whom the medical system has failed. I know they see chiropractic misadventures. I also know they used to teach Arrogance 101 to every incoming class and that it took a wise student to have an open mind. And in practice, they are too busy to make a phone call. But as the medical people try to convince the public that they are moving in the direction of alternative therapies, which patients are longing for, it would help for them to be curious and communicative.

In her keynote address the following fall at an integrative medicine conference that her staff has invited me to, Dr. Silva gives the introductory remarks and mentions how important it is that all of us communicate. That's good. And yet, the only communication opportunity we have so far, is an invitation to be one of ten "alternative healers" to sit on a panel, to be presented with case histories taken by M.D.'s — where we neither touch, see, nor converse with the patients — to give them ideas about how to create a care plan. There is no remuneration involved. It is such an insultingly bad idea that I do not return for the second meeting. At the same time, patients are led to believe that there is a new level of communication growing to serve them.

I'm glad I know how to hang out in an upside down yoga posture and breathe and relax — helps me with the ass-ended ideas of the day-to-day world.

Balancing has evolved over the years I have been doing it — a therapy that evolves with the consciousness; first, it was the individual relating to herSelf, then to another in a relationship, and often now it's about the person's relationship to the larger world.

Dorothy

KAREN: *Remember Ruby, Jane's mom, my sweet, kind patient for many years until she began to mentally fade away? That's how we met Jane and Donnie when they came back from Virginia so Jane could care for her mother?*

MARGARET: *I do. It must have been worth it because Jane and her mom were so close. But then, she and Donnie had to endure her dad's prejudice against their lifestyle, especially bitter when he gave the home place, the farm acres and the timber to her other siblings. Ruby was a Kinsinger, you know, and I think the wealth and the acres came from the Kinsinger side.*

Visitor parking at the Pleasantview Home is shady with trees in full, late-summer flourish. I slide from the behind the driver's seat and step into the Kalona ambience. It seems to arise from an abundant mix of well-meaning people serving their own, yet drowned in a full ladle of patriarchal gravy and superior attitude. Kalona, six miles east of Wellman, is a bigger community and surrounded for miles by Amish farms with their large families and the smells of active barnyards. I've come to the Home this afternoon to visit Dorothy Kinsinger.

Dorothy's been Karen's patient since we first opened our home practice. Back then Karen called me to treat some reflex points that would help Dorothy's sixty-eight-year-old knees. I met her lying facedown on Karen's table, her granite-gray hair pulled into a bun under her white covering. Perhaps the sieve-like mesh inhibits a woman's radiant light from shining too bright.

I grasped her hand in greeting and felt the warm, bony grip and sinewy strength of her farm-lady grip. "I'm going to massage some places on your hips and thighs," I said.

She gave a muffled merry chirp from within the headrest paper, "That's OK."

I massaged along her beefy thighs and along her spine on the flowered print of her cotton dress. I asked her to sit herself up. Her cheeks were reddened from the headrest. I showed her a few more points on her round belly and along her rib cage. When she was ready, Karen helped her slide off the table and back into her black, unshined shoes. She was not very tall and was a little tipped forward at the waist. She took a couple of tentative steps and then seesawed across the room with a startling gate. She turned and grinned, "That's heaps better! Now we're cookin' on the front burner!"

Dorothy became a monthly patient, and we got to know her bright expressions and uncommonly sunny personality. Often she came early for her appointment and sat at the top of our sidewalk steps with Willy Mays, who was out making his rounds. "My dogs would love you," she said in her own lilting purr as he arced into Halloween-cat posture, smiling with his eyes closed and nuzzling her skirt.

Joyful, sprightly, unsophisticated and unselfconscious, her soft brown eyes were buoyant behind black plastic and metal glasses. She was the youngest daughter who stayed home to care for her aging parents until they each passed. With no formal education and her parents gone, she worked with mop, broom and bucket, cleaning the Kalona Pleasantview Home so she could barrel her little brown sedan along the dusty back roads with independent aplomb. Typically, it was her brother who had the authority over the family's acres since Dorothy had no husband. I got the idea that, over time, the remains of those acres were lost to debt or the sucking black hole of agribusiness.

After we moved to the new office, we didn't see her at all. Someone told us that a mild stroke caused her to have an accident and drive her car into a ditch. She recovered in that same Home.

Then, a kind nurse from the Pleasantview staff calls the office. "Dorothy is a resident here again. Would it be possible for you to come give her a treatment?"

So here I am. I push open one of the double glass doors to the lobby, pausing to take in the subdued activity of elderly all-white inhabitants. Some walk, some roll, some walk arm in arm with a helper. Each is slowed or afflicted in a physical or mental way. Grasping my leather bag, I walk to the main desk. In the hub of phones, medicines, charts and generally cheerful demeanors, I introduce myself and ask for Dorothy's room. My reception is congenial and respectful. In this area, chiropractic is a longstanding backbone of community care.

"She's in this hallway two doors down on the right," says a tall open-faced, forty-year-old woman, gesturing behind me. "Just so you know, she's been emotionally upset for the last few days. You can go on in; she's expecting you."

I take a breath, straighten the collar of my cotton shirt and knock lightly on the partially open door. There's a muffled mewling coming from the bed. The window reveals a tidy, grassy lawn with trees and clumps of purple asters; there's a dresser beneath and an armchair nearby. On a credenza at the left wall, a row of black-and-white photos of solemn family members sits next to a soft riot of colorful stuffed animals. Dorothy is a fleshy plumpness among the pillows and appears to have been crying for days.

"Dorothy," I say, "Can I sit with you?" She nods and snuffles, her face a wrinkled tear-stained mess. I sit on her bedside. "Your Willie Mays sends his best."

"Ooohh!" she cries and tries hopelessly to smile at the same time. She blubbers something that I can't make out.

I take her hand in both of mine. It's cool and dry, unlike her face. I stroke the back of it and massage her hardworking forearm. "Let's talk about what we should do. Shall I adjust your neck and back?" She nods vigorously. "Then maybe we should use some acupuncture needles to calm you a bit." She nods again, eyes closed.

I rearrange her in bed so her back is to me, then gently adjust her vertebrae with Karen's adjusting instrument. She relaxes a bit. I massage the tense muscles of her neck and shoulders and arrange her once more on her back. Little trickles slowly weep from the corners of her eyes and I dab them with a tissue saying, "We'll have to keep your ears from filling with tears. Can I put a few needles in your arms and legs while you lie there?" A quieter nod.

"Why don't you take a few long, slow breaths, then you can tell me what brought all this about." I feel this might send her into another cascade of tears, but she takes a full breath and seems determined to get herself under control.

Her body softens into the covers as she relaxes and looks over, trying to find herself in her despair. She begins quietly. "It started with my accident." She squeezes her eyes tight to clear them. "Did you know I had an accident?"

It's my turn to nod. "Yes, I heard about it a few months ago."

"Well, I had to come to the Home to recover ... it turns out I had a little stroke which is why the car went into the ditch. I was in here for awhile, but not that long," she says, in a defiant tone. "Not that long. Not so long that my brother needed to move all my stuff out of the house and auction off everything but what's in this room. I begged him to wait, to at least let me come and see ... to say goodbye at least ... to have some say. But he didn't. And now it's all gone ... the house too ... the only place I've ever lived. I have to live with him and his wife."

I have unspoken opinions of these actions, of this brother solemnly shouldering his manly burden, ignoring his spinster sister's distress to get immediate control of the last of the money, forgetting that her care for their parents freed him to live his life. His picture is right here on the credenza.

"I'm sorry, Dorothy. That's a terrible blow." The needles are out now, discarded in my little plastic disposal container. I smooth the back of her now-warm hand, stroke her hair and tuck the blue stuffed bunny under her arm. "Can you rest now?"

She looks diminutive, but calm, and smiles a tiny crooked smile. "Yes, I think so. Here, just fill this in." She hands me a slightly rumpled check from the credenza.

"How about I look in on you next week?"

"Well, my brother will have to approve since he'll be paying."

Of course he will. And I notice Vernon's signature in my hand. "Sure. We'll just see then. Call any time," I say, and give her hand a little squeeze, laying it alongside her softened body. I slip back out into the gravy. The thoughts crash in again, my prejudices against oblivious, entitled men who are scornful of women's feelings and perspectives they view as weak sentimentality — practiced behavior as detrimental to themselves as it is to their relationships.

I see her several more times at the Home, maybe once a month, until the spring day the nurse calls to say they have to cancel her next treatment because

Dorothy is at University Hospital for a liver biopsy. I think *Yeah, little spots of fury.*

When I call up to see how she is doing, they say that she's back in her room but not fully conscious. I decide to drive up to the City to see her that evening. Entering the hospital empire, I navigate the acres of parking ramps, the maze of wings and "You are Here" maps to find her room.

The back of her hospital bed is propped up. Her hair is pulled back with no covering. She has on a much-laundered white-with-blue-patterns hospital gown. Someone has put her blue felt bunny under her left arm. Its bright eyes peer out to observe. Her hands repose quietly on her lap, hospital band around her wrist.

In the quiet, she is not vulnerable and distraught like at the Home. I abruptly feel something much more important is happening, like this is her opportunity to escape if she wants to take it or if some naïve do-gooder doesn't come along to interrupt the delicate process.

Urgently, but calmly, with all the time in the world, I say, "Hello Dorothy. It's Dr. Margaret. Your kind nurse at the Home told me you were up here."

No shift, no wrinkle, no response; just quiet restful breathing. "Willie Mays says hi as always. And the dogs wish you well. They miss you, but know you've got other things on your mind. I just came to tell you how Karen and I love you and truly understand the situation you're in." No change. Not a stir.

"So I came to visit you for both of us, just to let you know that if you want to take this opportunity to let go of this world, for a beautiful next one, we support you and completely understand." Her room and the hallway beyond are tranquil, the lights dimmed for evening's quiet.

"I know things took a bad turn for you. We want you to have your independence back and live in your joyful way. Whatever you choose, we want you to be heaps better!"

There is no sign that she hears me. I give her and bunny a hug and a tender squeeze of those quiet hands. I slip out and unravel my way through the glaring maze. Back in my car, I breathe deep and squeeze merciful tears from my own eyes as I drive the dark, quiet road back down to Wellman.

Her nurse at the Home calls the next day. Dorothy passed unexpectedly in the night.

I believe the goal of Balancing is to liberate and actualize the aspirations of the True Self.

Final Straw: The Pergola Incident

KAREN: *Don't you think that your excitable ideas are a little too much and are creating animosity?*

MARGARET: *It sure seems that way. But how can you compromise with willful hostility? I have to follow through.*

The long council table in the town hall and the familiar, but somewhat guarded, faces of the council members give my stomach a tiny ting of self-consciousness as Richard and I wait in the front row for our turn to present. We are the entirety of the Tree Committee.

Richard, master carpenter, divorced father of a teenage daughter, has returned to his hometown as a widower from a lengthy gay relationship in San Francisco. He assumes a likely celibate life, singing at funerals, working as a maintenance guy, occasionally trolling lonely byways on the internet and otherwise living in gray T-shirts and worn trainers. I appreciate his talent and lack of dourness.

We wait for the meeting to open. I twirl my pencil between fidgety fingers. My mind loops through a blur of my previously spoken words in this municipal arena. First, standing with other town citizens suggesting the town reconsider placing a shallow well three hundred feet, the minimum legal distance, from a toxic, antibiotic- and hormone-filled hog-waste lagoon; next, as Park Board president celebrating each member's

particular projects; then, resigning that very post, calling out Mayor Max for his costly bumbling and micro-
managing; and, most recently, another packed council
meeting honoring Wellman as a Tree City, showing pictures of some of the seventy trees we've planted around
town, some with gangly high-school seniors, others
with earnest sixth graders.

Now it's a pergola. I feel Karen rolling her eyes
in wonder at my dogged persistence. But she goes to
sleep at night and dreams colorful imaginative scenes
of shopping in fantastic places — at least when she's
not late for a test or lost in some building. What's in
her environment doesn't bother her as much. But me,
I often dream about fixing stuff. The first I remember
was in my early twenties when I awoke with an idea
for the perfect design for a piece of leather to repair my
softball cleats because my left foot had worn through
at the toe from stepping off the pitching mound. Or, I
dream about how to adjust an infant or design a recip-
rocal-motion chair bike. So, yes, now it's this pergola,
since the town is my current campsite, complete with
dysfunctional family members.

My circulating thoughts are interrupted with the
call for new business. I move to the end of the table
and scoot an oblong of cardboard the size of a TV tray
to the middle of the table. I smile my best in the face of
my audience's typical reluctance and avoid imagining
their thoughts. I remind them of Wellman's park pride
and their participation in this. A few jaws soften.

"This oblong represents our little park on the corner lot downtown," I say. "Here at the back," and I designate the short side near me, "is the alley separating it from the old phone company which has now become a branch of the Washington Federal Bank." Presumably, I observe to myself, to expand access to those millions of farm-subsidy dollars.

"This side to my right abuts the two-story, yellow-brick mural wall of Semler's Hardware. This other long side to my left is the Third Street side with street parking and good exposure for the farmers' market. The front shorter side is the Main Street side across from Freeman's Grocery. You can see the flower gardens along the sidewalk and the little walkway to the flagpole." I lean forward on one arm and point with my pencil to green magic marker blobs along the front side and the flagpole about a third of the way back.

I hear myself continuing, "Farmers' market vendors line up along the southern mural wall in search of the limited shade. The remaining vendors along the alley here are in the full blazing sun. We would like to propose a pergola along the alley here," and I point to the short edge nearest me.

I look at Richard. He nods. Then I reach down to my side into a paper sack and take out this little glued-together model that looks like popsicle sticks, lined up in parallel rows, on upright sticks glued to a pine board. I set the model at the end nearest me. "Here's the simple design. Eight uprights supporting front and back horizontal beams, parallel planks on top of them and a little bench seat along the back. There are ..."

I pause to remember, and Richard, pushing his metal-framed glasses up the bridge of his nose, smiles and croaks, "Twenty."

"Yes, right, twenty shading planks. As you look at them you can see that three end planks at each side are staggered to get progressively longer. They have soft ogee curves cut on their fronts." And now, the wrap up: "The point is two-fold. First, to create a welcoming structure to shade the farmers' market vendors and anyone who wants to sit here out of harsh sunlight. Second, to clearly mark the boundary between the park and the graveled area where the bank staff parks next to the alley. You know how gravel likes to creep."

Afterward, the members seem happy with the idea. They will take it under advisement and let us know. I'm attached to this idea because we've put a brilliant Japanese maple near the front of the park to contrast with a pyramidal pine tree and the yellow mural wall. There's a stately pin oak that will keep its leaves all winter in the open space. I clap Richard on the shoulder. This feels good.

Time passes, waiting for next month's meeting. Then I discover that, somehow, after the presentation there has been a groundswell of volunteerism. A bunch of guys got together and built their version of the park pergola. I only discover this at the Thursday farmers' market the following week when Mayor Max is doing what he does best, holding court and blustering under a structure that looks like a card table on stilts smack in the middle of the park's lawn. Too tall. Too square. The vendors and their wares still sweating in the sun. Are the volunteers happy with their accomplishment? Just impulsively had this idea, I guess. Like patients whom we tell something multiple times, then who walk in saying they had this great idea that they are going to start wearing supportive shoes. Except this is not really like that at all.

So what shall I do? Just let this ride? It's no-win, that's for sure. Now we are continuing on down that slippery slope of passive-aggressive behaviors that puts grass stains on my ass in my nice new jeans. Does our idea threaten their delicate little egos? All I know is, it is sullen, willful hostility, which trashes the park aesthetic and gives Mayor Max a vaulted venue to hold court. Richard is pissed about the terrible construction and design. He's a good radical in his heart.

We agree that we must go back to the council, giving the members a heads-up beforehand. We'll just say it must have been a mistake that they forgot there was an original plan or some complete crock like that. We will reuse their materials.

So we get our own set of volunteers. We could have made T-shirts or ball caps and drawn a line, but we just need to get this over with. We disassemble the deck on stilts, which is pretty easy since it's so shabbily put together. We dig holes and put in braces and cross pieces which Richard has precut. Three guys in overalls hoist and fasten the top planks. It looks good.

I've brought a cooler with beer for our group. As big hands grasp the cans and crack them open, making that wonderful little cluck-pop-fizz sound, we admire our handiwork. Then I tell them the story that old Ward told me about the $100 flagpole-painting incident. They laugh in appreciation of the originality. These guys are terrific in showing their support for doing the reasonable, wise thing. They do not likely have dealings with the other passive-aggressive "volunteers." Today I just love them for not being persuaded by meanness. There's tall, jovial Dean, the electrician; short, squat, laughin' and smokin' Billy from the phone company; and placid but quietly subversive Richard. I appreciate their solidarity and thank them for donating their discerning brawn to the project. Each one seems pleased to have been able to participate in something for the sheer joy in it. And now it's done.

And me too. I'm done. As I head home I recall my dream from this morning, just before waking — new and different from the fix-it, understand-it themes. In the busyness of the day, I had forgotten it. Now I re-experience its joy.

My hair whipping, blasted by wind. Leaning forward in earnest. Cheeks flexed under goggles pushing hard against my face. Focused ahead. Gripping a smooth, cunning motorcycle. Fast. Faster. Around a tight mountain road.

Ahead races a squirrel. A squirrel! I am following headlong, trying to keep up. She's easily outrunning me. Fast. Fast ahead.

No thinking, just driving. Steep curve. Climbing sharply to the right. Following hard. Road spirals out of sight. The squirrel flips her tail at the ledge. Leaps high and long. Body and tail extended in a long smooth arc. Beyond the cliff. Above the treetops. Into oblivion.

Time expands, then slows. Straighten the bike. Balance the handlebars. Stand tall on the pegs. Breathe deep. Jam the throttle down. Lean back and soar after her. Beyond the edge. Arcing. Higher ... Flying now.

Awaken. Hold the feeling. Infinite possibility.

Some people remark that they change so quickly after their Balance that it feels like open/free space in their heads, with no thinking.

Parking Signs and National Security

For over a month now, standing at attention in the little corner park across from our house, near the edge of its sunny green lawn, is a lonely metal post. It awaits its special parks-colored sign that supposedly will say, "Parking for Park Patrons Only."

MARGARET: *I'm making my own sign to screw on that post in the park since it's taking them so long to get the hassle started.*

KAREN: *Of course you are. What's it going to say?*

MARGARET: *It will be a thin wooden sheet the size of an ordinary No Parking sign, but I'll hang it sideways and paint WELCOME and a border in parking-sign red...easy for the average grade-school park patron to read when they are backing up their vehicles.*

A barrel-shaped, rugged-looking guy is standing in the clinic waiting room one morning when Karen comes out of her adjusting room, phone in hand, to check her schedule book. She covers the receiver and says, "I'll be with you in a minute." Continuing her phone conversation, she writes a name in the book, then turns to the newcomer. "You don't have an appointment, do you?" she says.

"No, I'm on my way to the university, but my brother said I should stop here before I go for the procedure."

"What procedure?" says Karen.

He blushes. In his fleece shirt, clean jeans and heavy leather jacket, he fumbles for words and says, "Well, I have to go to the..."

Karen looks at him closely. "I'm Dr. Zakar. Tell me your name and what's going on with you."

The words rush out. "My name is Steve Barnard. I have an appointment up at UIHC to get my left testicle removed. After a bunch of tests that were negative, they say that perhaps removing my testicle will relieve my groin pain that I've been having for the last month."

"If you can wait a bit..." she says.

He nods. The front door opens and in comes Jody, the wiry, joke-cracking night nurse. Karen slides a yellow intake form and a white "circle your pain" sheet into a clipboard and hands it to Steve with a pen.

"Here. Sit or stand, whatever's more comfortable and fill out these two sheets." Then she turns away from him. "Good morning, Jody. Come on in."

"Don't worry," says Jody, smiling and smacking her gum toward the new guy. "She can help." Entering the adjusting room, she continues, "I see they're putting up a No Parking sign just across the street from the clinic. I thought it was already no parking along this street because it's a state highway. Anyway, my neck's a mess after double shifts this weekend."

As all this happens out front, I'm in the quiet back room with the orbit-blue wall finishing last night's tacos and black beans, sitting with my feet on my desk. I've just made a presentation to twelve home-schoolers from Shiloh, teaching them the wonders of muscle testing. After the class one of the teachers steers her thirteen-year-old son over to me. Lance needs you to ask his body some questions," she says. "He's been beating up on his brother. Can you do that?" Before waiting for an answer, she turns to join the others getting ready for their next event.

"Hi Lance, now that you know how this is going to work. Put out your arm and say, 'I love my little brother Darren.'" I push. His arm stays strong.

"Say, 'I want to hit my little brother Darren.'" Arm weak. Hmm, he doesn't want to hit him.

"Say 'I have to hit my little brother Darren.'" Arm strong.

"OK, so you don't want to hit Darren, but you have to. Does that sound like what's happening, Lance?" I say.

He seriously considers this, then shrugs, "Yeah, I think so."

"Do you know why?"

His shoulders rise again, his arms cross in some unnamable frustration, then fall to his sides. He shakes his head.

"I see. You are doing something you don't really want to be doing. Do you think maybe you and your mom can work out why this is happening?" He nods.

We find his mom and let her know what we discovered. "If you two need any more help figuring out what's going on, let me know. We can have an actual session." I shake Lance's hand and hug his mother.

Now, sitting and chewing the last chipotle-flavored taco bite, I ponder the "I don't want to but I have to" concept of violence. Does that mean someone has been aggressing on him? Or that he's watching it happen to someone close to him? Maybe he can't say. Maybe this kind of irrationality rules the sociopathic mind. It's an interesting thought. But no time to linger, I wash my spicy hands and pack my teaching bag. I better get up to the City to teach another class, this time at Eastwind School of Massage.

Every couple months I come up here to teach. Today's class is basic kinesiology principles for an adult audience. It's an elective in the curriculum to expand the students' scope. My goal for the day is to create a consciousness about muscle testing and an awareness of reflex points for joint repair. After class, I stop by John's Coffee Place for a piece of lemon poppy-seed cake and a coffee for a reflective moment.

It's been a little over four years since our New Year's Day 2000/New Millennium/New Clinic Open House. Later that year George W. Bush became president with Sandra Day O'Connor's swing vote on the Supreme Court. The following year, on September 10, 2001, we returned from visiting our soon-to-be land partners in New Mexico. Immediately the next morning, our "from here" friends called to say, "Turn on the TV!" which we didn't have, so we could see the now-iconic pictures of planes hitting the World Trade Center and the tremendous rubble of their subsequent free fall. This has evolved to a war in the name of revenge and remembering this violent unrelated act. Now, we are preparing for another election manipulation.

I glance at the newspaper headlines pounding the push of war in Iraq and decide to cheer my mind by rewriting or creating them anew:

Condoleezza Rice Suggests Iraq Intelligence Wrong; Comforts Cabinet by Playing from Mozart's Piano Concerto in D-Minor

Dick Cheney Spotted with Actual Full Smile of Goodwill

Don Rumsfeld has Compassionate Dream, Retracts Torture Plans

George W. Bush Declares Free University for All: Mandatory Arts

Hillary Clinton Accepts True Calling as New York Senator

Iowa Senator Grassley Remembers His Roots, Vetoes War Appropriations

OK, it's time to drive home; the familiar hillsides, curve, four-way stop, turn west. I think that, in this time, our business just gets better and better. The referral base has reached a sixty-mile radius. If we didn't have our practices it would be seriously depressing. I'm finally making close to an educated woman's living by doing what interests me and not having to work for one of those bosses or administrators whom my clients need to Balance about.

When I visit the City, I see no evidence that the health professions have a plan to examine the politics of food or chemical agriculture unless you count the

Iowa Pork Producers funding the medical school's nutrition studies program. It seems there is a greater and greater divide between the Magic Bubble and the nether counties; between those whose jobs are well-funded and the people struggling with the loss of population, community and tax base. What fills that need for community? Could be it's this new talk radio? And the churches? Makes me think about my evolution professor who used to whoop about the ignorance of the creationists and brag about engaging them in intellectual fights, saying how unsophisticated they were. Creating another divided population where the elites can knock the saved; the saved can be more righteous than the elites. Can't see that it will end in harmony.

OK, here's our little outpost in our comparatively remote part of the empire. As I walk into the house Karen stirs from snoozing in her chair, "How'd it go?"

"Class was good. The owner dropped in during class. Nice, but he had to ask me the muscle relationship to the ileocecal valve in front of the class, sure that I would remember, but since I was so focused on presenting my material I just looked at him like a dimwit. Later remembered it's the iliacus. So ... Did you save your guy's precious jewels?"

"Too bad. And yes I did." She describes how she taught him to lie on his back, bring his bent knee to his advancing belly, probe over the front rim of his pelvis painfully and deeply into the fibers of his spasmed psoas.

"Did he cry? I cried when you did that to me."

"He had been crying in pain and for his limited options for a month. Anyway, it released enough of the torque on his lower spine so that, for the first time in more than a month, he was nearly pain-free. Better yet, I taught him how to treat it himself so he can take care of the problem whenever it arises. Especially because he's employed by the Feds and spends his days riding through the backfields of Iowa farms on horseback, looking for illegal pot. Just too much sitting."

We stretch out in the living room and brag a bit more about other patients we've helped. About Karen helping Brenda Bowman, after her T-bone car accident, finally get the appropriate oblique neck X-rays showing the disc blebs that needed to be surgically repaired.

"Her orthopedist had to send the results to me as Karen Zakar, M.D., not D.C."

And about Bonnie Morse, who had already had her neck fused. She required getting adjusted, doing her shoulder points, Balancing to accept that she did the right thing divorcing the man she loved because he was no longer capable of being a father and then buying a Buick sedan, whose vibration did not disrupt her neck's equilibrium. The fact that pointy screws from the plates in her vertebrae protrude into her spinal canal do not seem to worry her orthopedist, like they worry me.

"Oh hey, I have a Balance person for you," Karen says. A woman whose throat constricts and she gets nauseated every time she goes out to eat."

"OK, thanks. Sounds like you had a good day in the trenches." I bend to give her a goodnight kiss.

"Well, but, it now looks like they are planning to put No Parking signs on the cross street where our people park when the back lot is full. Probably because you've annoyed so many town guys."

"The cross street? That street is wider than any street in town. We must be a threat to national security. And by the way, those are the themes of this reelection campaign — national security and family values."

I would love to muscle test more sociopathic minds to see if there really is an inexpressible kernel of Love deep under their fearful hatefulness — though it's not a population that volunteers for Balancing.

Hog Pile

MARGARET: *Honey, after my best year ever, my business is falling off instead of continuing to grow.*

KAREN: *Repercussions from ... well, you know ...*

MARGARET: *Well, maybe. Not that they're my patients. This seems to be something different.*

KAREN: *Now that you mention it, my Shiloh people haven't been around for awhile.*

Back in chiropractic school, a fellow student told me about this guy who was a patient in the student clinic while he recovered from a work accident. He was a big guy, say 280 pounds, six foot six. Not huge in the Midwest but a big guy. His job was second station on the kill line at the wiener plant in Davenport. As my friend described it, hogs are delivered one by one in a line. The first guy makes the kill and sends the fresh carcass down a chute. The second guy, our guy, grabs the hog, takes his knife saber and slits open the hog's entire ventral side, basically from throat to genitals, then sends the bleeding corpse on into the bowels of the bologna factory.

On a particularly bad day for the patient, but sort of the inevitable outcome of such a job, he slipped and fell onto the chute, trapped under the hog he'd just gutted. No one realized his predicament and the line kept going. Another dead hog, slick and stinking with warm blood, landed on him. Then another. Then another. Covered in sticky coagulate, he could hardly breathe, limbs pinned askew beneath the weight of the load of carcasses. He was unable to move until, finally, someone down the line figured out there was a problem. Trapped. Powerless. A gory, slippery quagmire.

The helplessness of the guy to overcome the escalating immersion in bloodshed has stayed with me as a metaphor I've come to call Hog Pile.

Previously, my only reference to it was in a larger, more universal context, with each thud of duplicity in political or religious arenas, or with each carcass of daily life insanity — the diminished vitality of food, the casual tolerance of environmental poisons, the corporate crusade for our hearts and pocketbooks — slipping and sliding down the unequal playing field.

Until now. Now, we're tumbling into the Hog Pile. Stop the line! But, no one can help us.

It's late winter of 2005; Bush 44 has just begun his second term as president. We sit at the kitchen table, our uneaten meatloaf and homemade fries with peppers, onions and arugula pushed to the side with the organic ketchup. We nurse cups of sarsaparilla tea.

Karen breaks the quiet. "It's coming out now, that last year's Bush campaign about his support for marriage between opposite sexes — that it can't be 'severed from its religious, cultural and natural roots without weakening the good influence of society,' or some hodgepodge of words — was specifically designed to ignite the Midwestern evangelical Christians."

Thud.

"Well that sure worked. I'm also thinking it must be those two new guys on the council who are pushing these no parking signs through," I say. "One is the husband of the woman who officiated the Democratic caucus. I called her afterward to say what a great job she'd done and suggested she consider running for council. He was speaking to her in the background. I felt his dismay — a jealous conservative christianguy. Probably buying this antigay line ... surely not a Democrat.

"The other one is our neighbor who used to be so helpful and nice if I was having a car problem ..."

Karen interjects, "Maybe helping his gay son with a job referral in the City was too much. Dad has to admit that his kid really isn't going to straighten up. He might be a guilty parent, so he has to blame us."

"And the other council members are just letting them do it."

Thud.

We fall silent again as our dinners congeal on our plates and dogs gaze longingly toward the leftovers. Then, we remember the letter from two days ago. I had just brought in the mail. Two bills, a catalog, a pizza ad and a small handwritten envelope addressed to us. Not Drs. Zakar and Hansen; just juvenile handwriting to "Karen Zaker" and "Margret Hansen."

I slit open the envelope with my pocketknife.

"OK, this should be good. 'Dear Karen and Margret. My name is Rebecca Phillips. I am a senior at Iowa Mennonite School. Each student in our class chooses someone to pray for as our senior project. My friend

Amy Boswell and I have chosen to pray for each of you. We pray that you will find Jesus and take God in how you live your lives. In Jesus name comma Amen comma Rebecca Phillips and Amy Boswell.' Oh, for godsake!"

Karen looks like she's been punched in the gut. Her hands come over her stomach and she steps back in revulsion. "Pray for us! Those conservative Christians are so arrogant. Remember, they removed Leland from devotions class for teaching 'too much Love.' They need to stop with Leviticus, already, and get to John 13:34. 'A new commandment I give unto you, That ye love one another as I have loved you ...' There's some Jesus for you!"

We cradle our teacups, slumped in our chairs. I'm struggling to piece this together. "This means the teachers *and* the students *and* probably the parents are in on this. Judging our hearts."

"I've told you, my patients say that of late there has been specific preaching against us from the pulpit. Remember the woman from a few months ago who came to get adjusted after a fall? After a few visits, when she has recovered and is pain-free, she tells me I'm doing the work of the Devil! You remember? The work of the Devil! Some gall. I got out that Bible I keep in my desk and marched right out and shook it at her. 'You just show me where in this Bible it says that your Devil heals!'"

"That's right. I remember ... But these girls ..." I move now to sit on the harvest-gold countertop. "I guess if you rule their hearts and minds first, then it will be easy to rule their bodies later. Did they declare their virtuous plan to the whole class? Will they regret this later?"

Karen straightens up with her palms on the table. "Just last spring we had high school girls from the Mennonite school come and do work for us on their Community Service Day. They were friendly and helpful. We laughed together. But then this reelection campaign comes crashing into our community, unbeknownst to us, a divisive machine sucking up to single-issue voters, spreading hate for political ends, warping true relationships. Now girls learn to demean their role models. Fear suffuses the community.

"Meanwhile, our patients are occupied with their own lives with no clue any of this is happening ... I see no other way. We have got to get out!"

"I have to agree," I say. "I liked Wellman at first because of its independence — with its own bank, grocery, phone company, gas company and enterprising guys — plumbing, tires, electrical, cement. But, things are changing. This week I went into eighty-plus-year-old Harold Huntsberger's shop on an electrical errand. I watched while he rooted around in his anthropological dig and found a perfect cord for my fifty-year-old waffle iron. He charged me two bucks. How great is that?

"But, in the background the radio was on, spoiling our simple interchange. It was that soul-sucking dementor Rush Limbaugh sullying the airwaves ... sneering, blaming ... blaming you and me for everyone's problems. It was the first time I'd heard such a vicious backdrop to a public transaction. I had to wonder, even in our perfect waffle cord moment, what Harold was thinking and if he would be his kind self. It was alarming. And it's all around us."

"I even heard it when I went to the post office," says Karen. Then, reflecting another moment, "You know, taking a careful look in my schedule book, I see I haven't had a patient from Shiloh in over two months.

"When I think back, first there was the matriarch's daughter, then the daughter of our landlords, and of course Bryan, whose family I cared for in trade for construction projects, then the husband of another patient — they all felt comfortable enough to come out. But, now it's a complete reversal. Even Shiloh is sliding into gay phobia. Oops, we didn't mean it! Hide away again in your tattered closet, or move far away. Or, like Bryan's family, just rip it down the middle — two kids and a wife who hate him, two who support him. Their church has lost its way and is skidding down this repressive and autocratic slide — far from how they were evolving when we met them. If they'd been like this all along we wouldn't even have stayed!"

Thud. Thud. ... Thud.

It's the final collapse of the whole shebang.

Karen yearns for the people she has worried and anguished over to stand up for her. She has a depth of intimacy and understanding from caring for patients over the decades for injuries and regular maintenance. She supports them through pregnancies, treating the children, knows the husbands, teenagers, grandparents — their histories and interrelationships — been to births, weddings, funerals. She knows who has fallen from grace in the eye of the local Mennonite church, through pregnancy or pot-smoking — those evildoers. She keeps the hardworking guys from going under the knife, allowing a strong resilient healing. "Besides helping them recover, I've saved Blue Cross Blue Shield millions of dollars over the years." She knows the family dynasties do not concern themselves with the spineless people behind this offensive thinking. Still, it's a terrible crush that no one is able to come to her defense … especially me.

And, I didn't actually know I had gotten so miserable with the miserable community because I was so immersed in my own practice, navigating people's interior landscapes, stumbling upon a secret door to the Self's psyche. It falls open and I tumble in, looking round, wondering *What the Hell is this?* Here's the Self's interior mansion of ornate beautiful woodwork and gilded surfaces. But, instead of golden light streaming through the tall, holy windows, they're draped in cobwebs and bound by dripping ceilings and moldy floorboards from acquired, destructive beliefs. The Self's magnificent beauty — diminished by needing to be a guilty sinner to be saved, by having to suffer to know God or by learning either violence or helplessness from a loved one's abuse. Then, I discover the unspoken, astounding truth that everyone is capable of loving everyone.

When I finally awaken from my simplistic optimism, I discover that this instigated emotional carnage is splashed across our front door, running down the porch steps to the street and dripping a disgusting muck of pious insolence across the pretty, once-sunny windows of our clinic. This is well beyond a disagreement with neighbors that might resolve with a little coffee and conversation. This is a contrived shunning as though we are a menacing social threat. And, aren't we though? Supporting such blatant, threatening "gay" ideas like: Stop spraying your parks with nerve-damaging biocides. Or, suggesting you wear supportive shoes and keep good posture. Or, encouraging women to serve in community government while discouraging the continuation of an idiot running the town.

At the same time, this backlash has been calculated to wash over us, with no one specifically accountable except two ardent, foolish schoolgirls. That way there is no one to challenge, to talk back to or present the middle finger to. It's scaredy-cat hate, just so we know that we have no connection to them and are not part of them — never have been, never will be, never, ever should be.

And thank you for that clarity so we can leave you behind.

Our supporters — friends, patients from in and out of town and those who just go about their lives — seem powerless over this slime of orchestrated ostracism even if they know about it. And, of course, they can't know about it all — that slick of hatefulness slung again and again that now smothers our properties, our reputations, clogs our nostrils so we can hardly breathe, clots our eyes so we can barely see our way clear to get out.

We must retreat now and go fast to the property we bought with friends on a triple-rainbow afternoon on a quiet hillside in New Mexico.

Twenty years' work and commitment will slide away in the offal of this Hog Pile.

The pericardium meridian, the Heart Protector, is frequently treated in a Balance — tapped for a forgiving resilient Self rather than malignant, defensive prattle. The pathway begins in the chest, then advances down the front of the upper arm, to the inside of the elbow, down the middle of the forearm, across the palm, ending at the tip of the middle finger. It's possible that defense of Self is energetically advanced with the mudra of the extended middle finger.

We Can't Make This Beautiful

On the front porch of the cabin, we both sit drinking coffee, with our feet up on the railing, looking down the gentle slope to the grassy valley.

MARGARET: *It's sooooo quiet here on our sweet hillside in the cedars, piñon and scrub oak.*

KAREN: *And so fragrant after a rain.*

MARGARET: *I love our neighbor's little herd of cows in the valley with the kindly bull and a few babies ... and the morning klatch of mountain bluebirds down by the gate. I caught myself whistling this morning.*

KAREN: *I like that no cars pass since we're at the end of the lane.*

MARGARET: *Do you think I will ever have a new idea? Besides pitching moths into the webs of those spiders with abdomens as big as walnut shells, that is.*

KAREN: *That was my idea.*

The finish is quite a whirlwind. Patients are shocked. "You're leaving?" "Retiring?" "April twenty-ninth your last day?" "Where should *we* go?"

There is no one to buy the business so we are just throwing patients to the winds — to the applied kinesiologist and acupuncturists in the City or other chiropractors in the area.

A neighbor stops me to say, "Wow, you're leaving! Wish I had the nerve. I'll never get out of here."

The grocer says, "We'd hoped to build this business to sell, but no one wants to buy it, so we're stuck here." The tire guy says, "Nothin'll be the same around here."

Max Miller, Karen's tall, old farmer patient, called to make an appointment just after the first of the year — since he was still alive. "They told me up to the university that I had a year to live with this cancer, so I went home to die. But, since I didn't, I might as well get out and do something," he says. "And I sure do need a treatment. Helps my constipation."

During our last days he phones Karen, "Zakar, I just want to say thanks for all the good care over the years. I really appreciated it. Even though I always hoped I would go before you."

My Iowa City medical doctor friend, Karyn Shanks, who's been referring Balance patients over the years says, "When are you coming back to do Balances? I have space for you in my office." She, Leta, Karli and Lana, Jane and Donnie, Kay and Jeff, Fay and Ken and Leland all plan to visit us in New Mexico at 2 Glory Lane.

Karen leaves the clinic after her patients on Friday the twenty-ninth with no intention to step back inside. I can get this one. "Honey, I'm going to rent us a trash container for cleaning the yards and both garages. Can you stand it if we finally dump those boxes of your old class notes?" I have rearranged them in the storage room above the kitchen numerous times.

"Don't tell me about it, just do it. They were my life line."

"I know … even if you never once looked at them.

Say, do you like the new realtor?"

"He seems like a nice extroverted guy...from Washington so he knows this area. Wants all the walls painted a neutral color. We have a bank appointment to refinance one more time so we can pay off all the vehicles, including the truck and camper. Then everything's simple."

A stream of friends help clean, paint and pack glassware. Like a funeral, it's an astonishment how many participate!

Garage-sale and truck-packing day occurs the third week of May. That Saturday morning dawns cool and indifferent, then unfolds in ritual-like steps. Richard, my tree-planting comrade, and ever-supportive Kay and Jeff meet me out front of the office, where I've parked the rented thirty-foot Ryder straight truck. Richard and Jeff begin moving treatment tables, chairs, the front desk, speakers and artwork, packing with a spatial wizardry that crams our office into the front third of the truck. That is, after I give an expensive desk, rocking chair and my precious twenty-five-foot extension ladder to friends.

Up the hill, I repark by the Parking for Park Patrons Only sign. It's a final visitation for patients and friends on the front lawn. No looky-loos this time, except as they might be driving by, sneaking a last, triumphant, petty look. Our patient, friend and puppeteer, Teri Jean, serves coffee, brownies and little savory goodies. Kay joins Karen to sell and give away stuff. Her collections of CDs and jackets for sub-zero weather, vests, sweaters and shoes accumulate a pile of cash and make her friends happily nostalgic and warm for years to come.

The guys and I take a little coffee and refreshment break, not commenting on the breakup of our life all around us. Then, like pallbearers, they carry beds, leather chairs, dismantled worktable, bookcases, appliances and dishes and fit them in like we're building a bird's nest.

After cramming the household into the expandable truck, we swing down one more time to the garage behind the clinic — where this all really started — making something from the remains of Chester's worn-out, old-world life. I've already delivered my homemade bench from the clinic's front porch to Bill and Mary's farmhouse. Now, there's just enough room for the short ladders, tools, table saw and the last of Chester's ash, oak, hickory and walnut planks.

The truck door closes like a coffin lid over the remains of this saga. We head up once more to the final hugs, thank-yous and heartache moments of our lasting connections through time. Today's overflow of love and appreciation rouses us briefly from the wretched hollowness of the last few months.

Next morning, I begin the journey west. I wrestle the uncomfortable, clunky truck across the plains in a haze. When I notice, I remind myself to unclench my hands from the steering wheel and drive easy. Countryside, cities, truck stops glide by. I pass and am passed by all manner of summer vehicles. Nascent thoughts float just below my consciousness without taking form. Intermittent consoling tears escape from the corners of my eyes. This night, my sleep is deep and dreamless.

As I cross into the Land of Enchantment the next afternoon, nothing's a hurry. My breath is deep and free. Exiting the interstate onto a two-lane highway, I drive south into the Manzano Mountains, east of Albuquerque. Twenty-five miles and two country roads later, the truck shudders over a cattle guard onto Glory Lane — a single-lane dirt road — to our two-bedroom log cabin and separate five-sided flagstone building. It will be the new garage/shop, storehouse for the overflow of clinic tables and tools. It used to be the bar at the finish line of the half-mile lane where the previous owners raced their quarter horses. The neighbor's kids and cousins come to help unload our tightly packed belongings.

Night in the quiet, starry hills is a sudden vacuum. Unquiet, unformed emotions bounce off the cabin's log walls, even as I try to capture the certainty that somehow we'll figure this out. Next morning, with no time to linger, I reverse the two-day drive.

Back at the house, we efficiently cram the Ford pickup and camper full of Karen's clothes. I'll follow her in this rig as she drives the Volvo station wagon with cats, Dilly and Zoey, in the back seat, while Annie, the younger corgi, and Chica-Marie, the lovey malamute, curl up in the rear hatch. Murphy won't make this trip because Annie doesn't tolerate his snappishness anymore. She bit right through his ear last time they had a dustup. He's found a home with Karli and Lana at their tree-haven acreage with the chickens, guinea hens, miniature donkeys, cats and their two spotted dogs. He has a beautiful life, but I cry whenever I think of him — no more evening walks and snow angels on the golf course under the dome of heavenly stars. No more bright-eyed handsome boy.

Our properties are vacant, the yards pristine. Any evidence of our good works is gone, dispersed in others' memories. We wipe the miasma of Wellman's ick from our lips and shirtfronts to have a last hug before heading out in our separate vehicles. We'll overnight in Kansas and arrive tomorrow.

On this second trip through the voluptuous green contours of monoculture and sameness, I feel lucid and clear — gratefully putting miles between the *haters* and us. I had to look up *haters* in the Urban Dictionary. Turns out they're worse than people who don't like you. Apparently they have to take you down, especially if you appear successful. In this moment, we are unaware that we are not yet fully down: that several realtors will be complicit; that the next banker will collude in this mindset; that a final No Parking sign will go up in front of our house.

The church of hate and the politics of fear, like monocultures of the mind, will wipe out our resources. What we take now is what we will have — memories of those whom we love, all we have learned about our work and what we've got in those stacks of boxes as we dangle over the economic cliff to figure out how to survive.

What's the healer's response to all this? Beyond anger, disgust, humiliation and misery? Beyond attracting a new home and practice, and refinding ourSelves? One day, when I've quelled this tumult within, I imagine I'll have an answer.

That answer could be something like this. My recommendation for all these *haters* and their political shills is a steep, nonnegotiable financial punishment for scorning others and, concurrently, a permanent loss of any position of power. No whining, pleading, bargaining or sucking up.

And, what then? I like the idea of mandatory Hugging School!

I imagine that to consist of a long remedial sentence of compulsory cuddling and snuggling, learning unconditional positive regard. This might take lifetimes. Followed by classes learning soothing lullabies — not "As the bough breaks, the cradle will fall..." More like being "Enfolded in the arms of Infinite Love." Then, receiving a nepenthe for melancholia and fear while learning deep secrets of the Universe... something like that.

It's good we're moving on... Oh, and that I learned a few things.

I learned that these lazy hills and plains, suspended in the standing wave between two great rivers, were once a teeming grassland prairie with vigorous streams and wetlands. Incalculable numbers of teensy organisms within sweeping root networks assimilated water and minerals under radiant sun and starlight creating an immensely rich soil. And so, a delight of flowering plants, pollinating insects, creatures who fly, snuffle, graze, hop, paddle, skim, chomp, poop, trill and honk inhabited this generous nurturing universe.

But no more. These massive fields, mined of that intricate complexity, are now smothered in fertilizer, biocide and genetic reconfigurations. The diversity of species, now murdered, is evidenced even in my individual case study with no bugs splatted on my windshield.

Since the soil and the sea are mothers of the food chain, doesn't this land deserve an attempt at regeneration? It won't be millions of years of evolution, but why not give it a go? Even while adapting to a changing climate, imagine clear, contaminant-free creeks flowing to the rivers and the ocean, the rescue of species like the honeybee and perhaps revitalization and healing of the Dead Zone in the Gulf of Mexico.

Because that's the other thing I learned from watching patients repair, renew and reinvigorate. Healing is a direction, a journey, the innate course of life — freed in an instant when harm ceases.

As for you, Wellman? Good-Bye.

I'm glad that for a while we helped you live up to your name.

We just can't make this beautiful.

The Balance for treating past traumas does not appear to begin with forgiveness; it often begins with acceptance — that it happened to me and I was helpless to save mySelf.

You Mustn't Forget

KAREN: *I can't really say that you told the whole story.*

MARGARET: *I know. I left out how you held us all together for ten years till I could find my way and how searingly painful this ordeal was for our relationship. The whole story would take another twenty years. Everything's here, just sometimes a sentence represents a novel, a three-act play or a ten-thousand-word essay.*

KAREN: *Well, we have this place for the time being — even if we've got no recognizable life here yet ... And there are rattlesnakes.*

MARGARET: *You mustn't forget how many people you helped ... even if they were helpless to help us.*

KAREN: *But ...*

MARGARET: *They're just stories. Here, let me read you one.*

Recognition and Thank You

For design, details and a good eye:
Barbara Scott, interior design and format;
Helen Rynaski, editing; Gina Azzari cover design.

For advocacy, critique and a good ear:
Taos writing group, Bonnie, Bob, Pat, Lucy,
Sallie, Steve, Michael, Eileen, Elaine.

For dearest friendships and continual support:
Karyn Shanks, M.D., and the Iowa & Minnesota
Networks and Friends.

*For Love, insight and championing the
Life we have created:*
Karen Zakar, D.C., life partner and
companion, with dogs.

About the Author

Margaret J. Hansen loves to tell stories. She wrote *The Wellman Stories* because she likes you to be flushed with feelings — like the startle of paradox, like confidence in healing — particularly confidence in healing.

She has an undergraduate degree in Biology from the University of Iowa and a Doctor of Chiropractic degree from Palmer College of Chiropractic. Although she currently lives in Taos, New Mexico, she returns several times a year to work with her Eastern Iowa network.

As a white middle-class girl from the Midwest, many decades ago she had to discern and unlearn, among others, these three duplicitous teachings: Trust "progress." We are all the same. Be nicey-nice.

Find her at margarethansen.com.

Made in the
USA
Columbia, SC